Moses,
the Servant of God

Moses indeed was faithful in all his house, as a ministering servant, for a testimony of the things to be spoken after.

—HEBREWS 3:5

But the man Moses was very meek, above all men that were upon the face of the earth.

—NUMBERS 12:3

Moses, the Servant of God

Stephen Kaung

CHRISTIAN FELLOWSHIP PUBLISHERS, INC.
NEW YORK

Christian Fellowship Publishers, Inc.
New York

ISBN: 978-1-68062-087-0

Available from the Publishers at:

11515 Allecingie Parkway
Richmond, Virginia 23235
www.c-f-p.com

Printed in the United States of America

PREFACE

The life of Moses is most inspiring. At a certain point in that life he was called by God to be "My servant." Indeed, living for 120 years, Moses' servanthood was divided into three periods of 40 years each. During the first 40 years Moses tried to serve God according to his own way—which was the way he had learned from the world. So, during the second 40 years of his life, which was spent entirely out in the desert wilderness of Midian, Moses had to unlearn all he had learned previously, and also he had to learn God. Finally, throughout the entire concluding 40-year period of his long life, Moses was used by God as His faithful servant.

Let us see that, like Moses, in order to be able to serve God, we must first unlearn all which we have learned from the world. Then, and only then, can anyone serve God. A true servant of God must be selfless and be absolutely obedient to God. He may suffer incessantly from others, but he will be approved by God. And this is all that matters.

May we all learn to serve God as Moses did!

Contents

Publishers' Note

It should be noted that this series of messages was delivered by the author during the period from mid-April to mid-May of 1982 before a group of Christians who gather together for worship in Richmond, Virginia USA. The texts of these messages were recorded and later transcribed for possible future publication. It should be further explained that in preparing these transcribed messages for today's publication, this entire book's text has been extensively edited and that numerous additional Scripture verses—both texts and/or citations thereof—have been inserted here and there where deemed necessary or helpful to the reader.

Unless otherwise indicated,
Scripture quotations are from the
New Translation by J. N. Darby.

Chapter One

The First Forty Years

Acts 7:17-29—But as the time of promise drew near which God had promised to Abraham, the people increased and multiplied in Egypt, until another king over Egypt arose who did not know Joseph. He dealt subtilly with our race, and evil entreated the fathers, casting out their infants that they might not live. In which time Moses was born, and was exceedingly lovely, who was nourished three months in the house of his father. And when he was cast out, the daughter of Pharaoh took him up, and brought him up for herself to be for a son. And Moses was instructed in all the wisdom of the Egyptians, and he was mighty in his words and deeds. And when a period of forty years was fulfilled to him, it came into his heart to look upon his brethren, the sons of Israel; and seeing a certain one wronged, he defended him, and avenged him that was being oppressed, smiting the Egyptian. For he thought that his brethren would understand that God by his hand was giving them deliverance. But they understood not. And on the morrow he shewed himself to them as they were contending, and compelled them to peace, saying, Ye are brethren, why do ye wrong one another? But he that was wronging his neighbor thrust him away, saying, Who established thee ruler and judge over us? Dost thou wish to kill me as thou killedst the Egyptian yesterday? And Moses fled at this saying, and became a sojourner in the land of Madiam [Midian], where he begat two sons.

Hebrews 11:23-27—By faith Moses, being born, was hid three months by his parents, because they saw the child beautiful; and they did not fear the injunction of the king. By faith Moses, when he had become great, refused to be called son of Pharaoh's daughter; choosing rather to suffer affliction along with the people of God than to have the temporary pleasure of sin; esteeming the reproach of the Christ greater riches than the treasures of Egypt, for he had respect to the recompense. By faith he left Egypt, not fearing the wrath of the king; for he persevered as seeing him who is invisible.

We will recall that during the past few months we had fellowshiped together on the Bible's first book, Genesis, and we learned that Genesis is actually a book of biographies of eight men in particular.* We came to see that this book reveals to us that first of all, God is interested in man; second, that He is after the man of His own heart (I Samuel 13:14, Acts 13:22b); and third, that He is constantly working in the lives of men in order to bring them to be that man that will satisfy His heart. This first book of sacred scripture began with the life of Adam whom God, we are told, created in His own image (Genesis 1:27a), and concludes with the biography of Joseph, a man who throughout his life's circumstances repeatedly sat upon the throne as a king. And these two features have always been God's thought for man—image and dominion. Image speaks of the character and fitness essential for service in God's kingdom; and whenever the image of God's Son has been developed and matured in a person's life, that one is ready to enter into sonship. In other words, it is the placing of sons and daughters for the purpose of

---

* This series of messages was recently published and can be found in Stephen Kaung, *Men after God's Own Heart: Eight Biographies from the Book of Genesis* (New York: Christian Fellowship Publishers, 2017). —*The Publishers*

taking up kingdom responsibility; which is to say, to have dominion.

We often view dominion or rulership as that position in life wherein one is seated high above everyone else and ruling over them by issuing orders to people who obey them and who is being served by everyone. Not so! From God's viewpoint dominion actually manifests itself as service, and if people have been made fit to rule, they are able to serve both God and man. And that, essentially, is what is shown and demonstrated through those eight particular biographies in Scripture's first book.

Now in coming to Scripture's second book—Exodus—we have laid out before us the plan of God's salvation: it being illustrated for us in how God rescued the children of Israel out of Egypt so that they might be brought into the Promised Land, which is a picture in type of being brought into a life in Christ. It is a wonderful true story, and it reveals to us God's plan of salvation for fallen mankind. But for our purpose in these next few times of fellowship together in God's word we are not going to focus upon the history of God's people in terms of their deliverance and God's plan of salvation. Instead, I would like for us to approach the book of Exodus in terms of engaging in a biographical study of Moses, the servant of the Lord.

Now we know that sonship and servanthood are two of the great themes in the Bible—life and service. The kind of life a person has will determine the kind of service one has. If God can have a person of His own heart, then that one can be used by Him for His purpose. Hence, we are the children of God, but if we do not grow and mature in the Christian life, if we are not being transformed and conformed to the image of God's Son (Romans 12:2a, 8:29a), we cannot arrive at sonship. Yes, we may be children of God, but His purpose concerning us is that we should grow up into maturity as sons and daughters of God (I Corinthians 3:1, Ephesians 4:13 ASV, I Peter 2:2, II Peter 3:18a, Hebrews 5:13-14 ASV), so that He can place us with His

Son who is leading many such mature ones into glory (Hebrews 2:10a). Now if that is God's purpose concerning us, then we do indeed need to grow.

At the same time, however, we are not only His children, we are also His servants. Every child of God is a servant of the Lord. Of course, I am speaking in very general terms here. In other words, if we are born again into the family and household of God, then we are simultaneously called to serve in His house; there not being any exception. Every child of God is called to serve, yet sometimes we cannot or do not serve. It is not because we are not called to serve as servants of God; it is because we do not grow in spiritual stature, which hinders us from doing the work of God to which He has called each one of us. If we grow in the Lord, we shall discover that we are able to serve Him according to God's thought concerning each one of us.

Therefore, it is for this reason that after we have studied about the *man* whom God wants, then it seems to me that the right sequence in our fellowship together ought to be to continue with a consideration of the kind of *servant* God wants. And so, if we wish to study servanthood, then I think that apart from the Lord Jesus who is the perfect servant, our focus should be on Moses in the Old Testament and on the apostle Paul in the New Testament. Of course, there are many other servants of the Lord whom we find in Scripture, but I believe these two men are the kind of servants from whose lives we can learn a great deal about servanthood.

Numbers 12 relates what the Lord said concerning Moses: "… my servant Moses: he is faithful in all my house" (v. 7). And this divine commentary is quoted later in the New Testament book of Hebrews, chapter 3: "Moses, the servant of God, who is faithful in all God's house" (see v. 5).

Though the life of Moses is very full, in the Bible the Holy Spirit has seen fit to divide his life into three periods of forty years each. For instance, in Acts 7, part of which serves as a summary of Moses' life by the Holy Spirit through the mouth of the deacon Stephen, the Spirit as it were divides up the life of Moses into three periods of forty years each—forty years in Egypt, forty years in the desert of Midian, and forty years in the Sinai wilderness (vv. 23, 30, 36).

Every number in Holy Scripture has its spiritual significance, but the number forty is a very special one. It is a number conveying the idea of testing or trying. Four in Scripture is the number of man, ten is the number of responsibility; so by multiplying four by ten we have a number signifying testing or trying. We will remember that the Lord Jesus was in the wilderness being tested for forty days (Matthew 4:1-2). Moses climbed to the summit of Mount Horeb where for forty days and forty nights he waited to receive from Jehovah God the Ten Commandments (Exodus 24:18). The children of Israel were in the wilderness for forty years (Deuteronomy 2:7, 8:2). Accordingly, forty is the number conveying the notion of being tested or tried; and here in Acts 7 we are given to view Moses' life in terms of forty, forty, and forty; and during each period he was being tested.

The first forty years he was tempted or tested by means of the riches of Egypt; the second forty years he was tested by means of the dumb sheep under his care; and the last forty years he was tested by means of the stiff-necked people of Israel. It seems as though Moses had been tested and tested and tested, and the testing never seemed to come to an end. However, we discover that through all these testings a true servant of the Lord emerged; so let us not be afraid of being tested. We will be tested and tried to the very end, but thank God, at the conclusion of all such testings He will be moved to say about us, as He did concerning Moses: "My servant, so-and-so," and to conclude by saying: "Well done, wise and faithful servant; you can enter into the joy of the Lord" (see Matthew 25:21, 23). Oh, may it be so, indeed, with every one of us.

Now in our time together today I would like to share on the first forty years of Moses' life. He was born under an impossible set of circumstances, but he was born according to a definite purpose of God. Let us consider these circumstances. Moses was born under an Egyptian ruler who did not know Joseph, and we know this to be true not only from the Bible but also from secular history. It was at this time that another dynasty had come to rule over Egypt, and the rulers of this new dynasty did not know the story of Joseph—how God used him to save Egypt and the world of that day from starvation and death. Therefore, this Egyptian pharaoh, ruler or king did not appreciate the children of Israel as had the head of the former dynasty. And because God mightily blessed the children of Israel, they had grown to be quite numerous very rapidly, and hence the new pharaoh was afraid of this people. He thought that if there should be war with another nation or group of nations, most certainly the Israelites would turn against him and his dynasty and they would flee the country. As a consequence of this, he oppressed them and forced them into hard, even slave, labor. This new pharaoh made them build for himself cities and storehouses, but the people grew even more numerous. So he issued a decree that every male child born of the children of Israel must be cast into the Nile River and die. He wanted to wipe out the whole nation of Israel; yet, they continued to grow in number. We see, therefore, that Moses was born under the sentence of death. Or it may be said that he was born to die, not to live; for after he was born he was to be cast into the Nile River to be swallowed up by the crocodiles.

At this point in the narrative let us take note of something quite interesting. The Bible describes the baby Moses as follows: "He was a beautiful child; he was fair." I wonder if there is any baby who is *not* beautiful—at least in the eyes of the parents. I think every infant is beautiful; then why did the Bible describe this baby in such a full and emphatic way? For in Exodus 2 we read that when Moses was born, he was described as being fair (v. 2). Then, in Acts 7 we read that he was "exceedingly lovely" (v. 20)—which phrase means he was "fair to God."[*] And again, in Hebrews 11:23 the baby Moses is described as being "beautiful."

Why did the Holy Spirit draw our attention to this feature of this baby, and did so often? I believe the reason for this emphasis was more than meaning that Moses was a fair and beautiful baby *physically*; I believe that he was equally lovely, fair and beautiful to God in relation to His purpose. God had a definite purpose for this infant, in that He wanted to use him when matured and made ready to deliver the children of Israel. But strange to say, though God had such a definite purpose for that baby, he was born under what we would consider to be an impossible set of circumstances. In short, humanly speaking, Moses was born to die, in that there was no way out or safe exit from these adverse circumstances. Nevertheless, his parents saw that this baby of theirs was fair to God. Somehow they sensed in their spirit that this child was different from the other children, and that God wanted to use him.

Therefore, the Bible reads this way in relation to the parents: "By faith they hid the child for three months" (see Hebrews 11:29a). Yet, that was not an easy thing to do. For if the baby wanted to cry, how could they prevent him from being discovered? I think many mothers become exasperated whenever their child begins to cry, and they often do not know what to do. Moreover, everybody present will sometimes look at those mothers with annoyance.

By faith they were successful in hiding their baby for three months. That in itself was quite an achievement. But after three months they just could not hide the baby Moses anymore because he must have cried out louder and louder and more frequently, and there were spies everywhere. Therefore, they finally made an ark or basket of reeds and plastered it with a

---

[*] In fact, other English translations from the Greek original of this phrase have rendered it as: "lovely in the sight of God," (NASB), "a divinely beautiful child" (Williams), and "a beautiful child before God" (Beck).—*The Publishers*

mixture of pitch and resin. Then they put the little baby in the basket and placed it in the Nile River in accordance with the king's decree.

And God, in His sovereignty, led Pharaoh's daughter one day to enter the river's waters to take a bath and soon she saw the basket. She asked her maid to bring the basket to her, and when it was opened, again, God in His sovereignty caused the baby to cry, and that cry touched the heart of that woman. Although she knew it was a Hebrew baby, her heart was moved with compassion for this little one. So she took the baby to herself and had Moses' mother nurse the baby for her until he was weaned, and then the child Moses was brought into the palace (Exodus 2:1-10).

Moses therefore became the son of Pharaoh's daughter. He was not only allowed to live, he was also allowed to live in the palace; and the Bible declares that Moses became "mighty in his words and deeds." Mighty in words would indicate that he had absorbed all the wisdom and learnings which Egypt could offer; for at that time Egypt was the greatest empire in the world; and hence, Moses was given the opportunity to be educated in learning everything that there was to learn. Thus Moses became mighty in eloquence and great in wisdom, knowledge and learning. Moreover, according to historical tradition we are given to understand that Moses also became a great general in Egypt and that Pharaoh's daughter was herself considered to be a great woman in the Egyptian Empire. Thus Moses was well equipped and poised to succeed to the throne, he having become so "very great" (Exodus 11:3b). Accordingly, it could rightly be said that all the riches of Egypt were at Moses' disposal and that he was on the verge, as it were, of inheriting the world.

Yet, strange to say, somehow Moses eventually became restless; he was not satisfied and content with the cultural riches, wealth and power of Egypt. Somehow, deep down within his spirit an element of discontent was astir. This restlessness in its embryonic form had probably been planted in his little heart when his mother was nursing him. Somehow Moses' mother had put God into his heart, and now decades later God was drawing him to himself. For some inexplicable reason he felt that God was calling him, and hence he could not rest. A servant of God was sovereignly being chosen by God.

Just here, we need to pause for a few moments and inquire into this matter of God's sovereign choosing of His servants as revealed in His sacred word. In the story of Jeremiah we are told that when he was young, God spoke to him and said, "Even before you were born I knew you. Even before you were born I consecrated you. I have appointed you to be a prophet to the nations" (see Jeremiah 1:5). Again, in Galatians 1 we read what Paul said concerning himself in relation to God: "God … set me apart even from my mother's womb" (v. 15a).

Then again, in Ephesians 1 Paul tells us this: "God chose us in Christ even before the foundation of the world" (see v. 4). From these various verses we can discern that this matter becomes more and more mysterious: even before we were born God had chosen us; even before we were formed in our mother's womb God already knew us; even before the foundation of the world was laid, God had already chosen us in Christ Jesus. Though this is a mystery which we do not fully understand, yet we know from God's word that it is a fact. So far as Moses was concerned, even before he was born, God knew him. Even before he was born God had consecrated him. Even before the foundation of the world God had chosen him. Please take note here that Moses did not choose God; God sovereignly chose him to be His servant. And this is true concerning each one of us who have been born again by God's Spirit.

In considering this subject of servanthood, the first principle to be understood and grasped hold of by each one of us is quite simply this: God chose us. Please mark this well: You do not choose God, He chooses you, and He chose you even before the foundation of the world; He chose you even before you were formed in your mother's womb; He chose you even when you were in your mother's womb. Although you were not conscious of it, although you did not know anything about it, nevertheless, God has known about it all the time: He chose you to be not only His child but also His servant. Your having been chosen constitutes a sovereign, merciful and gracious act of God.

From the human standpoint it would seem as though the circumstances surrounding this little child Moses were arrayed against God's purpose ever being achieved for him because when Moses was born he had the sentence of death upon him and was destined to be cast into the Nile River and his life snuffed out. Furthermore, his having been reared in the royal palace of Egypt, where he had acquired all the intellectual and cultural riches, wealth and power the world had to offer, just did not seem to fit in with God's plan, will and purpose; yet He chose Moses. God's people may at times wonder how it is that though God has chosen them for service, many if not all of their circumstances would seem to be absolutely contrary to God's purpose in having chosen them; for their circumstances would appear to be the very kind which would lead them away from God and from the kind of service He has in mind for them to perform; nevertheless, *God* has chosen them!

Permit me to say that our whole concept of service is wrong. What I have in mind here is that in the service of God there is no such thing as volunteers. Oh, we may have been deluded into thinking that we have volunteered to serve God or perhaps into thinking that we can serve Him and that He should be honored because we have volunteered to serve Him. In fact, we may have been deluded into thinking that God should even thank us because we are willing to volunteer to serve Him. In *God*'s service there is no such thing! Humanly speaking, most servants on earth choose their master; but God the Master of all chooses all His servants. You do not choose God; He chooses you. And if He has chosen you, you have no way to escape His having chosen you.

We may recall a most revealing passage on service to God which Paul set forth in I Corinthians 9:16-17. Let me take up each short segment of it, one by one, and offer a comment on each. The apostle begins by stating this: "… if I announce the glad tidings, I have nothing to boast of." Here in so many words he is signifying that had he been a volunteer in God's service, his preaching of the gospel would have been that of which he could have boasted. But it having been revealed to him that God had chosen him for a godly service (see again his statements quoted earlier from Galatians 1 and Ephesians 1), his preaching of God's gospel was nothing of which he could boast. This Paul makes clear in the very next segment of this Corinthian passage, wherein he declares this: "For a necessity [or, compulsion] is laid upon me; for it is woe to me if I should not announce the glad tidings." Were Paul not to preach the gospel of God, it would bring a curse upon him. For in the next breath the apostle denies the entire notion of voluntarism when speaking of service to God: "For if I do this [gospel preaching] voluntarily, I have a reward. But if [this service] is not of my own will [and it certainly is not!], [then] I am entrusted with an administration [or, stewardship, to do so]." In other words, even if I did not wish to preach God's gospel, there has heretofore been committed to me a stewardship to do so as a consequence of my having been sovereignly chosen by God to serve Him. What, therefore, can I do? I *must* preach the gospel, willy-nilly. I *must* serve God.

I do hope we all can clearly see this. I do hope we all understand that we have not volunteered ourselves to the service of God. I do hope we can grasp hold of the fact that God has chosen us. Indeed, the Lord Jesus had himself made the same declaration: "You have not chosen me; I have chosen you that you may bear much fruit" (see John 15:16a). He has sovereignly chosen you and me, and because He has chosen us, we are under a compulsion, a necessity, to serve Him; and hence, there is no escape from it. If we serve God willingly and voluntarily we have a reward. Yet, even if we do not serve Him willingly, we must do so anyway because God has sovereignly chosen us. Now such is the very first principle of servanthood.

Allow me, if you will, to expand on this matter of our being chosen by God a few moments more. Yes, you are chosen to be a child of God, you must thank Him for that; at the same time, however, you are chosen to be a servant of His. In what capacity each of you is to serve, I do not know; nevertheless, you are a servant because you have been chosen. But do you thank Him for that? Or are you afraid of doing that? We are aware, are we not, that among unbelievers sometimes they do not agree with God but debate whether they want to be saved or not. On the other hand, too many Christians are debating the issue of whether they want to serve or not. Please understand, however, that you and I have no choice in the matter; you and I *have* to serve. As a matter of fact, every brother and every sister is called to serve.

Indeed, we need to take serious note of the following word of Scripture, a word which Moses would eventually take serious note of himself: "Let my people go that they may serve me." This was the command which God was to issue to Pharaoh through His servant Moses. In fact, because God had been working within the heart of Moses, this servant of His could not rest. Somehow, Moses sensed he had a calling to serve, for he came to realize that because God had chosen him, he had a calling from God to deliver the children of Israel out of Egypt. However, we find that Moses could not wait upon God for His timing and way of deliverance. Instead, when he had attained to the fully matured age of forty years, Moses, the would-be servant of God, made a decision on his own.

Which development now brings us to a consideration of the second principle of servanthood. As we have seen, the first principle of servanthood is that God sovereignly chooses you, and the second principle is that you choose God. Even so, we cannot reverse the order; nevertheless, there *is* the need for us to choose God; for notice what we read in Hebrews 11:24-25: "Moses, … choosing rather …" Yes, there is a choice we have to make, that is quite true, but please clearly understand that our act of choosing is not the first; God chooses us first. And because God has chosen us, therefore, so far as our personal experience is concerned, we shall one day arrive at a time when we must indeed make a choice—whether we shall choose God and His service or choose the world.

In this very connection, then, when reading the complete passage in Hebrews 11, we find that Moses made his choice: "By faith Moses, when he had become great [that is, when he had grown up (ASV)], refused to be called son of Pharaoh's daughter; choosing rather to suffer affliction along with the people of God than to have the temporary pleasure of sin." Upon his attaining the age of forty, Moses had to make a choice between the people of God and the pleasure of sin, to bear the sufferings of God's people or to enjoy the pleasures of sin. He had to make a choice between the reproaches of Christ and the riches of Egypt, Christ or the world, suffering or the pleasures of sin.

By this time in his life Moses, in the words of Exodus 11, was looked upon by Pharaoh's servants and by the Egyptian people as being "very great" (v. 3b); he had the world and the power over it almost within his grasp. In fact, he had been destined to be the future Pharaoh ruling over the world's greatest empire of that day. He had already proven himself mighty in both words and deeds, successful in having become a great statesman and a great general, and even poised to become an empire builder. All this had become quite evident in Moses' life. On the other hand, there was now before him God's service, which would mean for him to serve God's purpose by serving the children of Israel who were hated by the Egyptians. And were he to do that, it would mean that he would have to suffer with them. In short, it would mean either bearing the reproach of Christ or enjoying the power, riches and pleasures of the world. Moses had to make a choice, and it took forty years to bring himself to make that choice. As it turned out, at the end of those forty years, Moses the servant of God cast his lot with God and the people of God.

Why did Moses do this? We are told in the book of Hebrews that it was because he saw "him who is invisible"; and so, by faith Moses made that choice. Notice, too, that once having made that choice, he could have canceled himself out at any point thereafter and returned to the palace, but Moses never did. By faith, this servant of God saw Him who is invisible and remained faithful to the very end in his having chosen God and His purpose.

Please understand that there is no contradiction between these two principles of servanthood and the particular choice involved in each: God choosing us and we choosing Him. Let us clearly see that so far as God's eternal purpose is concerned He chooses us, but so far as our response to God's purpose is concerned we choose Him. There will come a day when you will have to make that choice; there is no neutral ground. Are you going to live for yourself? Are you going to build your own empire? Are you going to be successful in the world? Or are you going to live for God, serve His purpose, do whatever His will may be for you, in order that His people may be built together and His kingdom may be furthered? Each of us has to make that choice.

It is quite true that we each may not have all the potential which Moses had, but we each of us nonetheless have our particular world with which we each must come to terms; and hence, in principle it will be just the same. I wonder how many of us have already made the choice. On the other hand, I wonder how many of us are delaying that choice. I wonder, too, how many of us are still weighing these two realities in our individual worlds and do not know what to do—we being half for God and half for the world. When it comes right down to it, we none of us who are believers can do that. There is bound to come a time in our Christian walk when we have to make the choice. And there is no denying that it will be a critical moment.

Whom will you serve: God or mammon? (Matthew 6:24) yourself or Christ? Now it is true that so far as your fleshly-self is concerned, if you choose Christ it may mean reproaches are inflicted upon you, it may mean sufferings. On the other hand, if you choose the world, that may mean the pleasures of sin and even possibly the power, riches and cultural treasures of Egypt. Are you therefore going to be short-sighted or will you be far-sighted? Do you see the Invisible One or do you see all which is visible in the world? If all you see is the visible, the seen and the transitory character of this world, then without a doubt you will choose Egypt. However, if what you see is the unseen, then what actually is the world? To you it is but rubbish, refuse. Indeed, Paul himself made this latter choice. Said he on one occasion: "For the excellency of the knowledge of Jesus Christ I consider all these things of the world as rubbish and even filth" (see Philippians 3:8), and I for one would declare that he made the right choice.

If we read the pertinent Scriptures carefully, we would have to conclude that it was not an easy choice for Moses. In fact, I believe he went through many heart searchings and experienced many nights in which he could not sleep; yet somehow, the love of God constrained him (cf. II Corinthians 5:14a). And when he was forty years old, he cast his lot with the people of God. He made his choice—and it was the right one.

I believe Moses' decision was not unlike the decision which the kind of slave singled out for mention in Exodus chapter 21 ended up in making. We are told there that if a Hebrew among the Israelites became so poor that he sold himself to another Hebrew, he would serve him six years as a slave, and on the seventh year he could go out free. But if that slave loved his master and loved being in his master's house, he could say to his master, "No, I want to remain forever your slave." In that case, this slave would be taken by his master to that home's doorpost and have his ear pierced using an awl, and the result of this act would serve as a sign thereafter that this slave would remain such to that master for the rest of his life. And thus, this one would be no ordinary slave but a slave of love—a love-slave (vv. 1-2, 5-6). In a very real sense that is what Moses became: God's love-slave.

This is what needs to happen to every one of us. One day we, too, will need to tell the Lord: "I love You, I want to stay with You, and I want to serve You. I am most willing to have my ear pierced and become Your slave of love forever. I choose You as my Master and Lord."

I know without any doubt that God has chosen all of us who have sincerely received His salvation in Christ; but I wonder how many of us, in the words of Hebrews, have arrived at the point in our Christian life of having "chosen Him rather than ..." I do not believe that any Christian can ultimately live a life which is half-hearted in character, which is either/or in nature, or is a half-way existence. A believer in Christ has to make a critical choice. However, in order to make the *right* choice, faith is required. The Christian needs by faith to see the Invisible One if he or she is going to make the right choice. As we have further seen from Hebrews concerning Moses, he by faith "chose rather ..."—he having seen "him who is invisible." Such, then, is the second principle of servanthood: having been chosen by God, we choose Him and His purposes.

Now if a person has come into the position of being a servant of God, what can be said to be the primary sign of a servant or of servanthood? And such will constitute the third principle of servanthood. In the case of Moses, he manifested an interest in God's people. When he was forty years old, there came into his heart a desire to look with concern upon the condition of his brethren. We know, of course, that before this desire had surfaced Moses had lived in a palace, having lived royally because he belonged to the Egyptian royal family. And even though his brethren had been suffering a long time as slaves, he had not shown any concern about them. Moses was only concerned about himself: what he could achieve, how much he could enjoy, how much he could gain for himself. He was out to gain the whole world, and that alone was his concern and his interest. However, once becoming a servant of God, Moses for the first time became interested in what God was interested in. He felt concern about the people of Israel because they were the people about whom God was concerned.

So how do you know that you are a servant of the Lord? How do you know that you are in the place that you may begin to serve? I think the primary sign is that you become concerned and interested in God's interest and God's people. That is a sure sign of servanthood. Before that, you were interested in yourself or perhaps you were very much interested in your family (and of course you should be). Or you were interested in your business, in your future; but one day when you begin to be concerned about God's people—His church, His kingdom, His righteousness—then you will know you are to serve.

Let us be clear that service to God is not a work which is put upon anybody. Such service will be that which grows out of the heart's concern. In this world work is what is put upon you such as employment in a company or a business; and as such you are not concerned whether that company or business prospers or fails since that is the concern of the owner. You are just an employee who simply performs work and receives wages; and thus it is a work which has been put upon you.

However, in the service of God it is very different. In God's service there is nothing put on anybody; rather, service comes from within. By which is meant that God has put a divine burden in you; He has placed a divine concern and an interest in you. Indeed, it is His interest, His concern, His burden; and as the burden grows within you, you come to realize that it is service which God has called you to perform.

Now we find that Moses began to be concerned; it was as if he said to himself: "I live in the palace and my brethren will end up dying. Hence, let me go and see how they fare." So he went out to see what he could do. Unfortunately, Moses began this work independently. The burden was right, the concern was right; but instead of waiting upon God and letting Him take the initiative in showing him what to do and how to do it, out of his good heart Moses went forth to see what he could learn of the people's situation and determine what he himself could do to resolve it. Sure enough he was tempted again and again to do whatever he himself could do.

He went forth, and the first thing he found was an Egyptian ill-treating and beating a Hebrew. He looked to the right and to the left, and not seeing anybody in view, he beat the Egyptian to death and buried him under the sand. Since he had been mighty in deeds, Moses therefore thought his brethren knew that God was using him to deliver them. In fact, I think that night Moses probably slept soundly because he thought he had been used by God. Thus he was serving Him well, so he thought.

The next day Moses went out again and another temptation came his way to do something on his own. Two Hebrew men were quarreling and one was oppressing the other; so Moses, having been mighty also in words, began to use his eloquence to solve their quarrel, he saying to them, "You are brothers, you should not fight." He thought they certainly understood, but he was wrong. One of them pushed him away and said, "Who made you our judge? Do you want to kill me like you killed that Egyptian yesterday?" Moses thus became aware that the news of his activity had spread, and even Pharaoh, he now feared, had heard about it. So Moses fled for his life, he having become a complete failure. Yet we must thank God for that!

If you do not consider yourself a servant of God, you have absolutely no interest and no concern regarding God's people,

God's church, or God's interest. You will only be thinking of yourself and trying to build yourself up. But once you begin to respond to God's choosing of you and His call upon your life, then you will become concerned about God's people and interested in whatever God is interested in; and hence, if I may couch this in New Testament terms, you will begin to sense a responsibility concerning the brethren in the church of God. Thank God for that; for this is what every child of God *should* be concerned about.

However, a common problem usually arises, in that after you begin to be interested and become zealous for the Lord, you feeling warm towards Him in wanting to serve Him by doing something for Him, instead of waiting upon Him and allowing Him to show you what He wants you to do and how you are to do it, you follow your own natural instincts and simply launch forth and do it. And the result is that as He did with Moses God allows you to fail. For it is you who are taking the initiative, it is you who begins to speak out, it is you who begins to work the matter out; but the problem is that it is all emanating from your flesh. Yes, you may be mighty in words and in deeds, but oh, how terrible is that mightiness! Your heart is right, your intention is right, but your way is wrong. The good which you can do is actually very little; but like Moses at this moment, you can cause lots of trouble. And this is what is often to be found among God's people.

I would pause here to say, however, that it is my hope and prayer that all of God's people would rise up and be active; everybody in the church ought to contribute, do his or her part, and take up responsibility. That is what it should be in the house and family of God. Every believer's talent should be used—the five-talents believer, the ten-talents believer and the one-talent believer (see Matthew 25:14ff.). Every believer's talent should be brought into play, and if this is the case, we shall see the church greatly grow. But if brothers and sisters in the church are not concerned and end up letting a few brethren take up the whole responsibility, then those few will work themselves to death—that is most certainly true.

Now that is the nature of the problem when only a few in God's church are interested in pursuing God's interests. However, a very different problem arises in the church when *everybody* becomes interested and involved. What do I mean by *this* development? Well, if every member in the body of Christ becomes interested in assuming responsibility, what unfortunately may ensue is as follows: This one offers a word about a given church matter and another voices a different word; or a brother issues his opinion and a sister offers her opinion; in fact, everybody is quick to offer an opinion on this or that matter confronting the church. Many discussions occur, such discussions going in this direction and that; this one agrees, that one disagrees, and still another declares that this way is better while yet another states that a better way would be this way or that; even someone may assert that he does not see how this can be done in such-and-such a manner, but someone else may interject that the matter ought to be done in a different way. All these various opinions, views, and assertions come forth most readily, so that instead of the brethren waiting upon the Lord to know *His* mind, everyone in the church gives voice to his or her mind. That is what often, if not always, can occur when all the brethren manifest their "mightiness in *words*"!

Yet please be advised that this problem manifests itself not only in words but in deeds as well. By which is meant that when everybody becomes interested in God's interests and are desirous of taking up responsibility in God's house, what likewise can occur is that there is a display of the "mightiness in *deeds*"! Within that context you will find that church brethren are not at a loss for engaging in numerous activities which they undertake on their own. This brother is ready to do this and that sister is eager to do the other thing. Indeed, there is no lack of brethren, on their own initiative, undertaking to serve by doing this, that, and the other activity. Not unlike Moses, however, the end result is that a most unpleasant consequence, such as an Egyptian being beaten to death, occurs, or that a dispute between two brethren cannot be resolved; with the would-be problem-solving brethren in the church fleeing from the situation. In fact, these brethren had become so disappointed and frustrated over the fact that other brethren in the church failed to understand those who had gladly taken up responsibility to help. "God has called me," one of them might say, "and yet this is what I get for having responded to that call. God should have backed me up and prospered my efforts in serving Him. Instead, others in the church failed to understand that God has called me to serve, and they even rejected me!" And so, this one ends up thinking to himself: "Henceforth, I shall not ever again lift a finger to help out—I shall not do anything; even if God's house is on the verge of collapsing; let it collapse! From now on, no one will ever see my face any further, for I'm finished attempting to serve in responsibility among the brethren." And so, not unlike Moses, this one and that one soon flee the scene entirely. Once again, this is what can often occur when all the brethren manifest their "mightiness in *deeds*"!

Nevertheless, please understand that this is the way we learn. Nobody is born to be a servant of the Lord without the need of learning. There is no such thing as a spiritual genius. We all have to learn the hard way. Yes, it may very well be that not only brethren will not understand us; it may also seem that God does not back us up. Yet that is a further lesson we will need to learn if we wish to be God's servants—that He does not want us to serve Him according to our way, our wisdom, or with our strength, since His work can only be done by God himself. Unless we are willing to go through death and be resurrected, we are of no use in His hands.

Indeed, this latter observation points up what I believe is a necessary fourth principle of servanthood, which has to do with the cross. We have to learn the lesson of the cross in its working upon our flesh and cutting it off. It is those failures and disappointments and despairs in ourselves by which we are delivered from our flesh-self. Unless we are delivered from ourselves we cannot be used to deliver any brother or sister from himself or herself. Unless we are delivered from ourselves we cannot be used in any work of God because that would mean we would be doing our work, in our way, with our strength, and for our glory.

On the one hand, we need to rise up, give ourselves to God, and be willing to serve; on the other hand, we need to expect the cross to work in our lives and let our flesh be struck down lest our hand, like Uzzah of old, touch the ark of God (see II Samuel 6:3, 6-7). It would seem to be a paradox, and yet this is the way in which God will prepare His servants.

I do hope we can clearly see and understand these various principles which must govern servanthood. Everyone is a servant according to whatever his or her talent and capacity may be, and this the Lord knows all about. And hence, we all must serve. Serving the Lord is to be the hallmark of our life. We serve the Lord with the life which He has given us. So let us bear in mind these four principles: 1) God chooses us, 2) we choose Him, 3) God's interest becomes our interest, and 4) the cross has to be learned and applied to our flesh. And if these be true of us, then we shall find that through all these trials, temptations and testings God is able to produce servants who will really serve His purpose.

Shall we pray:

Our heavenly Father, how we praise and thank Thee that it is Thou who hast chosen us, not we who in the first place have chosen Thee. Our Father, we do thank Thee that we who are weak have been chosen to serve such a great God and merciful Master. It is our honor to serve Thee. Oh, our Father, we do pray that we may be so constrained by the love of Christ that we may give ourselves to Thee and say, "Lord, we do not wish to go out free because we love Thee. We want to serve Thee for life." And Father, do teach us the lesson of the cross so that as Thy word has warned us we may not serve Thee in "zeal without knowledge."* We pray that we may not touch Thy ark with the hand of flesh. We pray that Thou wilt deal with us by means of the cross so that our service may solely be *of* Thee, *through* Thee, and *unto* Thee. In the name of our Lord Jesus. Amen.

* cf. Romans 10:2.—*The Publishers*

Chapter Two

The Second Forty Years

Acts 7:29-35—And Moses fled at this saying, and became a sojourner in the land of Madiam [Midian], where he begat two sons. And when forty years were fulfilled, an angel appeared to him in the wilderness of mount Sinai, in a flame of fire of a bush. And Moses seeing it wondered at the vision; and as he went up to consider it, there was a voice of the Lord, I am the God of thy fathers, the God of Abraham, and of Isaac, and of Jacob. And Moses trembled, and durst not consider it. And the Lord said to him, Loose the sandal of thy feet, for the place on which thou standest is holy ground. I have surely seen the ill treatment of my people which is in Egypt, and I have heard their groan, and have come down to take them out of it; and now, come, I will send thee to Egypt. This Moses, whom they refused, saying, Who made thee ruler and judge? Him did God send to be a ruler and deliverer with the hand of the angel who appeared to him in the bush.

Exodus 3:1-14—And Moses tended the flock of Jethro his father-in-law, the priest of Midian. And he led the flock behind the wilderness, and came to the mountain of God—to Horeb. And the Angel of Jehovah appeared to him in a flame of fire out of the midst of a thorn-bush: and he looked, and behold, the thorn-bush burned with fire, and the thorn-bush was not being consumed. And Moses said, Let me now turn aside and see this great sight, why the thorn-bush is not burnt. And Jehovah saw that he turned aside to see, and God called to him out of the midst of the thorn-bush and said, Moses, Moses! And he said, Here am I. And he said, Draw not nigh hither: loose thy sandals from off thy feet, for the place whereon thou standest is holy ground. And he said, I am the God of thy father, the God of Abraham, the God of Isaac, and the God of Jacob. And Moses hid his face; for he was afraid to look at God.

And Jehovah said, I have seen assuredly the affliction of my people who are in Egypt, and their cry have I heard on account of their taskmasters; for I know their sorrows. And I am come down to deliver them out of the hand of the Egyptians, and to bring them up out of that land unto a good and spacious land, unto a land flowing with milk and honey, unto the place of the Canaanites, and the Hittites, and the Amorites, and Perizzites, and Hivites, and the Jebusites. And now behold, the cry of the children of Israel is come unto me; and I have also seen the oppression with which the Egyptians oppress them. And now come, and I will send thee unto Pharaoh, that thou mayest bring forth my people the children of Israel out of Egypt.

And Moses said to God, Who am I, that I should go unto Pharaoh, and that I should bring forth the children of Israel out of Egypt? And he said, For I will be with thee; and this shall be the sign to thee that I have sent thee: when thou hast brought forth the people out of Egypt, ye shall serve God upon this mountain. And Moses said to God, Behold, when I come unto the children of Israel, and shall say unto them, The God of your fathers hath sent me unto you; and they shall say, What is his name? what shall I say unto them? And God said to Moses, I AM THAT I AM. And he said, Thus shalt thou say unto the children of Israel: I AM hath sent me unto you.

Today I wish for us to continue focusing our attention upon the life and biography of Moses the servant of God. And we saw in our fellowship together last time that the Holy Spirit, through God's word, has divided Moses' life into three periods of forty years each: forty years in Egypt, forty in Midian, and forty in the Sinai wilderness. And we also saw last time that during that first forty years Moses had absorbed into his mind and soul all the secular wisdom and learnings of Egypt he could imbibe as a member of the royal household in Pharaoh's palace.

At that time, of course, Egypt was the foremost and greatest empire in the world. And the civilization, the culture, and the learning of Egypt were well regarded everywhere in the known world of that day. One need only look at the pyramids today as evidence of what a cultured and learned civilization it indeed was. Even today her great and accurate architecture is considered to be a model; and such architectural creations like the pyramids were built back in those ancient times, and during part of this period in Egyptian history Moses was being prepared according to God's sovereignty and purpose.

We learned last time how God in His gracious and merciful sovereignty rescued him from the sentence of death when he was but a babe and sovereignly placed him in the Egyptian palace, and for forty years he learned all the learnings of Egypt. In fact, it could be said that Moses was the most learned person in the whole world at that time. So much so that being mighty in both words and deeds he tried to use all such acquisition to save the children of Israel by his mightiness in all he had learned. But as we saw previously, the result was that Moses ended up a total failure. As a matter of fact, he had to flee for his life from Egypt, and for the next forty years he found himself having to tend a few sheep belonging to his father-in-law, Jethro, in the land of Midian.

Now if you were to place yourself in his sandals, I think you could well imagine what happened during those first few years of Moses' experience tending those sheep; for he had lots of time to think, and he must have been thinking, "What went wrong with me back there in Egypt? Certainly God wanted to use me to deliver the children of Israel, and I was trying to do it as best I knew how, and with the best I could do; and yet, not even my brethren understood, nor did God back me up. What went wrong?" Moses must have gone over those past incidents again and again, trying to figure out what went awry. Then, too, he must have waited before God continually, praying a prayer such as this: "If I have failed Thee once, give me another chance." But year after year went by until forty years had passed, yet nothing happened.

In Psalm 90, which was written by Moses the man of God, he declared: "The years of a lifetime are three score and ten, and if, by reason of strength, they be fourscore years." So far as Moses was concerned, he reckoned that the lifetime of a person would normally be seventy years, and if one were strong enough, he could reach the age of eighty years. In his mind eighty was the limit to a man's length of life. And here he was having already spent forty years in Egypt and forty more years in the Midianite desert; hence, Moses was now eighty years old, and therefore, according to his own estimate, this meant that he had arrived at the end of life.

It is my belief that during Moses' forty years spent tending Jethro's sheep he went through an unending process of having to unlearn everything which he had learned back in Egypt. Yet, in view of the outcome of those forty years in Egypt, this process was in reality a wonderful thing if Moses were ever to be used by God in future. For what he had learned in Egypt was the reason for his failure. Had he not been a learned person, had he not been so mighty in words and deeds, he might not have been a hindrance to God, and probably God could have used him back then. But because he was so mighty, because he was so learned, and because he had acquired so much worldly knowledge, therefore, he ended up a failure. God could not use him.

We might assume how good it would have been had God not given Moses the opportunity of learning all the worldly ways of Egypt. Why, then, did God allow him to acquire all the learnings of Egypt and thereafter sweep it all away and conclude by saying, "I cannot use you, Moses, because of all that you have acquired"? Is that not most strange? Indeed, it would seem to be a paradox. On the one hand it was God's sovereignty which made it possible for Moses to acquire all the secular wisdom and learnings of Egypt; on the other hand, these very things which he had diligently acquired became a hindrance preventing God being able to use him. Consequently, it would become necessary for Moses to unlearn all these things were he at last to be usable in God's hands. What a paradox, indeed!

Let us look into this matter more deeply. If you, like Moses, were to spend forty years with a few sheep, your acquired eloquence would soon be gone because there would be no one to talk to. Were you to talk to those dumb sheep, they just could not and would not understand. So Moses, after spending forty long years with those sheep, ended up unlearning and letting go of all his eloquence. Accordingly, no wonder that when God called him, Moses said, "I cannot speak," and that was very true: he could not speak. Then, also, in those forty years in Midian Moses had unlearned and relinquished all his mightiness in deeds. Back in Egypt he had been a great warrior and had become strong physically in his arms; so much so that he could even beat an Egyptian to death. However, when tending sheep such mightiness would be of no use: you have to be tender with them and handle them very gently. Therefore, after forty years Moses had likewise unlearned all his mightiness in deeds. In fact, when God called him to return to Egypt, he responded with, "Oh God, please call somebody else; I cannot do anything. There is nothing I can do." It may be very difficult to learn, but I think it is even more difficult to unlearn.

Yet Moses unlearned everything which he had learned back in Egypt.

I would ask again why in God's sovereignty does He allow us to learn lots of things but then require us to unlearn them? In order to answer this question it may be helpful to lay before us a few truths which can be of assistance in better understanding the explanation when it is given. Even before you and I came to know the Lord, He knew us. Even before you were saved, all your past was known by God. He arranged your past and allowed you to be in a certain family. God in His sovereignty also allowed you to learn many things in and of the world. But do you think because you have learned a lot, therefore, you can serve God? On the contrary, it is because you have learned a great deal which in itself disqualifies you from serving Him.

If, in your attempt to serve God, you depend upon what you have learned and what you know, and if you do so on your own, using your cleverness, knowledge and strength, you will discover that all of this is not only not a help but it is a hindrance; and you eventually shall realize that God will most certainly reject all of this and will declare, "I have no use of you with these things." And your response will quite naturally be: "Why, then, did You allow me, oh God, to learn all these things and acquire all these abilities?"

I believe that the explanation is quite simply this: that God has allowed you to learn and acquire these things so that one day you might unlearn them, yet not in the sense that you *forget* them but in the sense that you will not depend on them anymore but—and if I may use some New Testament terminology here—allow them to go into death and be resurrected for subsequent use in God's hands.

And so, let us now apply this explanation to the case of Moses. God wanted to use Moses to lead—not merely a few people but—a whole nation out of Egypt and through the Sinai wilderness into the Promised Land of Canaan. While in the Egyptian palace during the first forty years of his life Moses must have learned all there was to learn about government, administration, military knowledge, and the politics of that day; and because he had all this talented background, one day God could use him to lead out an entire nation of people. God could not entrust such an enormous task in a person who had never had such a background with a nation.

Similarly was it in the case of the apostle Paul, whom God used so mightily. Half of the New Testament was written by Paul because he was a highly learned Pharisee. God would be able to use these cultural abilities and talents of Paul's, but unless first they go down into death and are then resurrected, they are useless to God.

Natural talents, education, experience—all such accomplishments—are useful to God but only after they are unlearned. If, however, a person learns them but they are never unlearned through the death experience, there is no doubt that that person will depend upon these achievements to serve God. Do realize, therefore, that God has no use of anyone's natural talents, education, and experience if they have never been dealt with by the cross of Christ and been resurrected for their use by the Master.

Be advised, therefore, that God will use one's natural talents, one's education, and one's life experiences; but He will only use them after that person has unlearned them in self-denial. Only when a would-be servant of God arrives at the realization in his or her life of acknowledging and saying in utmost sincerity—"Lord, I do not know a thing; I will let go of all these talents, achievements and experiences; I let go of my pride in any of them; these abilities are absolutely useless unless You want to use them; and if so, then help Yourself to them and use them as You see fit"—only *then* can God use what He has allowed that person to learn previously, because they will then no longer be his or her idols. Instead, they will be useful instruments in God's hands.

God therefore allowed Moses to fail. On the other hand, what if God had allowed him to succeed in beating to death that Egyptian and reconciling those two brethren of his? Simply put, the answer is that Moses would never have been able to deliver the whole nation of Israel out of Egypt. Yes, he might have been able to accomplish a little here and a little there, but that is all he would have been able to achieve; he would not have been able to undertake successfully that which God had wanted him to do: which was, to deliver an entire nation from oppressive servitude under the Egyptian Pharaoh.

Consequently, here is an important principle for us to recognize and understand concerning servanthood. We must be willing to learn whatever God gives us the opportunity to learn. Let us not adopt the mentality: "I will not learn or experience this or that since it is of no use to God; so why waste my time acquiring it?" That short-sighted mentality is not acceptable, for let us benefit from the example of Daniel, whom when but a youth God put in Babylon for the purpose of learning all the ways of the government and administration of the imperial Chaldeans. If God should grant us the opportunity, let us learn everything we can; but let us also be ready to unlearn all such things.

Let us return to the example of Paul again. In Philippians 3 he wrote: "What in my former life experience I considered as gain ..." And what a gain it was! He was a very learned Pharisee, and knowing the law according to the righteousness of the law he was blameless, he was perfect; but he went on to declare this: "What I considered as gain I now reckon as loss." In order for Paul to gain Christ it was not only a matter of dross, it was also an immense loss. Dross is a serious enough price to pay in terms of prestige and reputation, but loss is far more than dross because it means the relinquishing of everything formerly deemed worthwhile to possess. Yet the apostle declared: "I consider all these things as loss because they hinder me from gaining Christ. I would rather let go of everything I personally valued most highly in order that I might gain Christ. Oh, to gain Christ and to know Him more fully is far, far better!" Hence, Paul was more than willing for all his learning, talent, and experience to be put to death if that meant the gaining of Christ in resurrection life. For did he not also write the following?—"That I may know Him (Christ), and the power of His *resurrection*, ... being made conformable unto His *death*" (see vv. 4-11, emphasis added).

Let us, however, take note of the fact that after the apostle had experienced the death to his self-life and the gaining of Christ in resurrection life, God could greatly use what he had considered to be loss. Thus, it can be said that, when considered in New Testament terms, Moses during his forty years in the backside of the desert experienced the letting go of everything he had learned, gained and accomplished back in Egypt—he had to unlearn all he had achieved during the first forty years of his life. And that is a vital spiritual process which we, too, must experience if we are to be usable by God as His servants.

Furthermore, by means of his forty years out in that same Midian desert Moses also experienced something else which was vital for him to come to terms with: that additional experience brought him to a point whereby he was able to truly know himself. Today people know a great deal about many things. They even possess an immense knowledge about outer space, yet do they really know themselves? Actually, not very many; for them this is an unknown. How can we truly know ourselves? Moses, for example, could not know himself in the Egyptian palace. And why? Because there in the palace his ego was so boosted, nourished, and inflated that he came to view himself as being somebody great—in modern parlance, as being a big shot. Actually, however, he did not know himself.

But out there in the quiet of the desert with only a few sheep to keep him company, Moses began to see who he really was. And what he discerned about himself was not that he was the adopted and favored son of the daughter of Pharaoh, ruler over the vast Egyptian empire, but that he was a good-for-nothing. Moses began to see himself as he truly was, and after those forty long years in the desert he ultimately came to the conclusion that he—now eighty years old—was as good as dead. For in his estimation age eighty meant the end was very near.

Any sense of ambition and hope were now gone. No longer was he ambitious to accomplish anything as before, and, furthermore, he had given up all hope that God would ever use him or that he could ever *be* of any use to Him or to anyone else, for that matter. To sum up, Moses considered himself as one dead, as one who has been reduced to zero. "Who today am I? I am nothing." He saw himself as being so nothing that he even tried to convince God of this self-estimation: "God, You cannot do anything with nothing. Send somebody else. Do not send me because I am just nothing." Thus did Moses come to know himself.

This is a lesson which every servant of God must learn: to know oneself. You who would be God's servant, allow me to emphasize that it is not enough just to know the Bible, it is not enough just to know the methods, ways, and techniques of the spiritual life; you must know yourself. If you do not know yourself, if you do not see yourself as God sees you in yourself, you are of no use to Him. But thank God, out there in the deserted Midian wilderness Moses learned to know himself—a knowledge which he could never have come into possession of while he was in the Egyptian palace.

You come to know yourself when you have been reduced to a position of little or no importance, when there comes your way difficult circumstances, failures and/or afflictions. These situations will help you to know yourself. If you have never been afflicted, if you have never suffered, if you have always been on top of every life situation—there being no failure, affliction or suffering—you will never know yourself. And though these may be difficult and in some cases extremely trying circumstances for you, do realize that they all have been allowed by God to occur in your life for one very good reason: that you may truly know yourself and, now knowing yourself, you may be able and willing to humble yourself before God.

Besides this, furthermore, Moses also learned to know God. In the Egyptian palace he did not know Him. It is quite true that he had a feeling or sense that God had called him. Probably his mother had put that feeling into his little heart when she was nursing him as a baby, but aside from that we have no proof that Moses actually knew God or had ever met God before. But in the quietness of his forty years spent on the backside of the Midianite desert under Mount Horeb he began to know God intimately. And let us be clear here that to be a servant of God the knowledge of Him is not only basic but is most essential.

Let us suppose that you do not know God. If you know the Bible and its techniques of inquiry, or if you know God's people and you even know yourself but you do not know *God*, how can He possibly use you? Such a thing is impossible! In the case of Moses, however, during the forty years which he would spend in the desert of Midian he would eventually be brought face to face with God in his experience of the burning thorn bush. Having been taken away from man, away from the multitude, away from the hustle and bustle of life in society, there in the desert quietness Moses was brought face to face with God Almighty, and so he came to know Him in His heart and in His ways and purpose.

Hence, it would not be incorrect to observe that that vision of the burning thorn bush, which event we shall consider more fully shortly, served as the consummation of what had been taking place in Moses' heart and mind throughout the entire second span of forty years in his life. It can therefore be said that Moses' mature knowledge of God in His many and varied facets—His very nature, His heart, compassion and mercy, His will and His purpose—did not spring forth all of a sudden but was the result of those many years of solitude in the Midianite desert, during which, little by little, Moses personally commenced knowing God. And this lengthy process of his in coming to know Him reached its culmination for him in his experience of the burning bush that was not consumed and which brought about his encounter with God face to face. Indeed, as we shall soon come to see, this climactic event likewise served as the conclusion to all which Moses had to unlearn and learn back throughout the course of those second forty years of his life.

Now as was pointed out before, Moses had by this time arrived at the age of eighty. He considered himself to be good as dead. All his ambition and hope were gone, and he was quite content to live a shepherd's existence and end his life doing that. But one day as Moses was leading his sheep to the backside of Mount Horeb, he noticed a thorn bush that was burning. Now in the desert a thorn bush is a quite common sight everywhere, but because there is a lack of water one seldom, if ever, finds an oasis where trees are able to grow. Why, though, are there thorns on these bushes? We are told that thorns are nothing more than aborted growths. There should be leaves, flowers, and fruit coming forth on these bushes, but because there is not enough water for nutritional growth, whatever little growth there is is arrested and hence finally aborted, and thus there emerge nothing but thorns.

So in the desert there are all these thorn bushes. They are not trees but bushes, and they are full of thorns whose growth has been aborted. They are very common to see in the desert. And because these thorn bushes are so dry from the lack of water and from the sun being so hot, it is a common sight to see these bushes suddenly catch fire by themselves. One would not need to use a match to ignite them because they will ignite by themselves. So, suddenly such a bush will display a flash, then burn, and finally be turned into ash very quickly. It is a common sight to behold in the desert, and Moses must have witnessed such a scene thousands, perhaps even ten thousands of times during those forty years in the desert wilderness. It was therefore nothing to excite the imagination. Consequently, on that particular day as Moses approached the vicinity of Mount Horeb and beheld a thorn bush begin to burn it meant nothing out of the ordinary to him at first; but then he noticed that *this* thorn bush was not being consumed in the least. Such a sight as *that* was indeed out of the ordinary; in fact, it was nothing less than a vision from Jehovah God. A most extraordinary vision was given to Moses that day at the most unexpected time and under the most unexpected circumstances.

Do we not think how wonderful it would be to be given a vision? "Oh, that God would give me a vision!" Now if God were to grant you your request, what would you be expecting? You would be expecting something spectacular, something tremendous, even something extraordinary. Yet, oftentimes God grants a vision to His servant by means of the most common, everyday occurrence—that which may have occurred every single day in that servant's life; nevertheless, on one particular day, such an ordinary occurrence may this time take on a different appearance: the very same phenomenon which had heretofore happened day after day after day turns out to be quite different in its appearance—Behold, God has granted His servant a vision!

Yes, that thorn bush which Moses caught sight of that day was at first burning like all others he had seen before, but this one turned out not to be reduced to the nothingness of ash but continued to burn without in the least being consumed! Why so, wondered Moses to himself. And hence, he drew near to that bush to see if he could discover the reason why, and as he approached the spot where the bush was, a voice came forth from the thorn bush. Why so? It was because the Angel of Jehovah was dwelling in the thorn bush! Whereupon Jehovah God called to him, saying: "Moses, Moses!"

And Moses replied, "Here am I." From this response we are given to realize that at this point Moses definitely knew God. For if Moses had not known Him he would not have been able to recognize who it was and then to say, "Here am I." He truly recognized the voice of God here. And it can therefore be concluded that this event and this vision constituted the consummation of these forty years spent out in the Midianite wilderness. God then declared to Moses: "I am the God of your fathers, the God of Abraham, the God of Isaac, and the God of Jacob." Upon hearing this, he trembled in fear and hid his face for he was afraid to look at God. The Lord next said, "Take the sandals from off your feet, for this is holy ground." And there God further revealed His heart to Moses—on this occasion concerning His people. God explained: "I have heard the cry of My people. I remember My covenant, and I am sending you to deliver My children out of Egypt into a land flowing with milk and honey."

Forty years ago it had come into Moses' heart to go out from Pharaoh's palace to see and even to show sympathy towards what had happened to his brethren. It was a good intention, but it was his own. Another forty years later, however, he was given a vision of the divine heart, and accordingly God sent him forth. By this latter time, of course, Moses had come to the conclusion that he would never be sent, that he had given up any hope of being sent; but let us understand that the end of man is the beginning of God. And by this time in his life, Moses had truly come to his end. *Our* problem though is, that we do not come to our end. If one day, however, we truly come to our end—period!—that will be the day on which God shall begin. So God's beginning with Moses commenced by His giving him a vision of a thorn bush that burned and burned and continued to burn.

Let us consider this vision more closely. In this vision there were three elements—the thorn bush, the fire, and the Angel of the Lord, and in this event these three are brought together as a whole. Now the vision may be applied individually or it may be applied in a corporate sense. By which I mean that one may apply the implications of this vision to Moses himself or to the children of Israel, the latter of whom would be the subject of Moses' work; nevertheless, both applications are appropriate.

Let us first discuss the application of this vision on the personal and individual level. Do let us see and deeply understand that this thorn bush represented the man Moses, and that, dear brethren, is very humbling. While Moses was in Egypt, he looked upon himself as being like unto a gigantic cedar tree on the summits of Lebanon (cf. Judges 9:15, II Kings 19:23, Psalm 29:5, Isaiah 2:13, Jeremiah 27:5).* Oh, he deemed himself to be someone great, and as a matter of fact, the whole nation of Egypt considered him as such (Exodus 11:3b). He had become a great man towering over the rest of the Egyptian empire's inhabitants; after forty years in the desert of Midian, however, he viewed himself as nothing but a consumed thorn bush: "I am not a tree; I am a mere bush. I do not bear any leaves, blossoms or fruit; I produce only thorns, and thorns, I realize, are a sign of curse."

Allow me, if you will, to ask a question: Do you see yourself as a thorn bush? Have you caught the vision which Moses saw? If you have truly received divine vision, you will readily discern that the world is but a desert—dry, barren, scorched—and that you in yourself are not a tall, impressive cedar tree situated atop the summits of Lebanon but are no more than a useless thorn bush unfit for anything but to be burned and consumed, that you are nothing as a result of the curse pronounced by God in judgment upon fallen mankind, and that you in and of yourself do not and cannot produce any fruit for God. A thorn bush is good for nothing because it burns up so quickly; consequently, it does not even give off enough heat to warm the desert traveler. And that is precisely what you and I

---

* One Bible commentator has noted that the cedars of Lebanon "are almost always used in Scripture to illustrate strength, stability, and majesty. … Evergreen [cedar] forests graced the mountains of Lebanon," with their trees reaching up to heights of as much as 100 feet.—Dennis Moles.—*The Publishers*

are. Therefore, if we are ever to be true servants of God, we must first of all have vision of what we actually are in ourselves, that we are nothing but thorn bushes, and like those thorn bushes we deserve no other outcome but to be burned up—that is to say, to be brought to the end of ourselves.

In this connection, however, we must not leave the matter there, with its negative though quite necessary outcome; for there is another and very positive facet to this vision of the thorn bush. Yes, it is quite true that fire in the Scriptures speaks of judgment, for we read in God's word that "the wages of sin is death" and that "it is appointed to all men that they should die, and after death the judgment" (see Romans 6:23a, Hebrews 9:27). Moreover, we also read that we are all under the curse of the law and that when the law is being carried out, that spells for us judgment and a being consumed (cf. Galatians 3:10-13).

Nevertheless, and here I would point out the vision's positive aspect which was mentioned a moment ago, if we have not been consumed it is due solely to the mercy of God. This is because fire not only burns and consumes, it also can purify and sanctify: it will eliminate everything which can be burned; but if there is that which cannot be burned, it will be purified and even glorified. Indeed, to describe this purifying process in New Testament terms and apply it to ourselves individually, it can be said that because the Lord Jesus is in us, the fire does not consume us but only purifies and sanctifies us, so that whatever is of Christ becomes brighter than ever before; and it is in that strength and power that we, as was Moses, can be sent forth to do the work of God.

Paul, in fact, has given us a classic illustration of this in his First Corinthians epistle: Whenever gold, silver or precious stones go through fire, he explained, they will be refined, purified, and even glow; but if the material is wood, stubble or hay, such will be burned and suffer loss (3:11-15). We see, therefore, that in the process of judgment, fire exerts a purifying power as well—it can purify even to the extent of glorification.

That thorn bush out in the Midianite desert was supposed to have been consumed, and yet, what a sight it was for Moses to behold: a thorn bush continually on fire without ever being burned up and turned into ashes; on the contrary, the bush was even aglow and giving forth a brilliant shining appearance! Was that not wonderful?!? And the explanation for this lay not in the thorn bush itself but could be traced only to the One who dwelt in the bush—even the Angel of Jehovah, the Angel of the Lord. Now let us be very clear here, that in every instance in which the Old Testament speaks of the Angel of Jehovah or of the Lord, such always refers to the second Person of the Godhead—even to the Son of God, the Lord Jesus Christ (see, e.g., Genesis 31:11-13; Hosea 12:3-4 explaining Genesis 32:24-25; Judges 2:1-4; Zechariah 3:1).

At this point I would have us notice and consider how Deuteronomy chapter 33 describes one characteristic about God at this time: "... him that dwelt in the bush" (v. 16). Think of that! Yet we are also told in the Scriptures that God dwells in heaven: "the heavens are My throne and the earth is My footstool; what is the house which you would build for Me? and what is the place of My rest? But I will look upon those who have a broken and contrite spirit, those who tremble at My word" (see Isaiah 66:1-2). Even wise King Solomon acknowledged that the heavens and the heaven of heavens cannot contain Him (II Chronicles 2:6a), and yet He dwells in that person whose heart is broken and whose spirit is contrite. God humbles himself to dwell even in a thorn bush; He humbles himself not merely to visit it, but to dwell therein, to make His home therein!

Now that is the gospel, is it not? The gospel of Jesus Christ is essentially this: that the Lord God the Almighty, the Holy One, should choose to dwell and make His home in humble men and women such as we (e.g., John 17:23a, Galatians 2:20a, I John 3:24). He not only visits us; He makes His home in us who—by comparison with Him—are nothing more than thorn bushes. What a great and gracious God! And it is because the

Angel of the Lord "dwells in the bush," therefore, the judgment fire of God cannot consume the bush but purifies, sanctifies, and even glorifies it.

Oh, when Moses beheld that vision, he could verily see himself as that thorn bush. He, as it were, could envision the fire consuming him himself, but surprisingly, he was not consumed because God was with him. God was there alongside Moses, even within him, purifying him by burning up all the rubbish in him, all the dross of himself which needed to be consumed; yet at the same time God was nonetheless glorifying Moses by His being within him. It was altogether a most glorious sight, and it thus gave hope to Moses.

And were we to apply this thorn-bush vision corporately to the entire nation of Israel, we are left with the same picture. In that sense, the nation of Israel can likewise be viewed as a thorn bush. For consider her situation there in Egypt. The Israelites were not even allowed to live; indeed, it was the intent of Pharaoh that the whole nation was to be annihilated; accordingly, it could accurately be asserted that this people was nothing more than a thorn bush whose very existence lay under a curse. In fact, the judgment of death was upon them; nevertheless, somehow this nation—like the vision's thorn bush—would not be consumed because God was with her people. God used purifying affliction to bring them back to himself. And hence, that constitutes the vision corporately.

Oh, how we all need that vision! Everyone who desires to serve God must have vision. Indeed, we are informed by Scripture that without vision people will cast off restraint, that without vision people will perish, that without vision there can be no sense of direction in one's spiritual life, no strength or sustaining power, and no unity (cf. Proverbs 29:18a). All who wish to be used by God must experience the implications—both negative and positive—of this vision which Moses received. You must see yourself as the thorn bush. You must see that you deserve nothing but to be consumed. However, somehow God miraculously preserves you because He is in you, He is with you, He is purifying you, He is glorifying you so that He may use you. If you see and understand the implications of this vision, you will never boast of yourself. As a matter of fact, it is foolish to boast. You will never try to share in God's glory because it is His glory, not yours.

But you must also see the content of this vision as it relates to the corporate work which God wants you to undertake. Consider the children of God today in terms of the body of Christ. She in herself is that thorn bush—possessing no beauty of her own, a dried-up entity having nothing of which to boast. The church as you see her today should die, for in her weakness and multiplied failings there is no reason for her to continue; yet the church has continued to exist for two thousand years. And why? Solely because the Lord God is there in that thorn bush, corporately-speaking. He is using afflictions, sufferings, persecutions, problems and troubles of all kinds in order to purify His church so that her Lord and Head may present to himself a glorious church that is ultimately going to be without spot or wrinkle or any of such flaws and imperfections (Ephesians 5:25b-27).

Unless you make it a point to catch that vision, there will be no motivation for you to work in serving the Lord. This is because, failing to catch that vision, your attitude will be that the church is destined to die; therefore, let her die; indeed, you will assume that she does not deserve to be rescued. If, however, that vision is yours, then by faith you will realize that God is going to have a glorious church; and because of that realization, you will go forward to serve Him in this task of doing your part as His servant in helping to build up the church despite all adverse circumstances. For with this vision there comes God's commission to His servants. For did He not instruct His servant Moses, "You must go"?

If, of course, you lack a divine vision, you will have no commission. Yes, you may be commissioned by man, but you will have no *divine* commission. However, like Moses, once you have been captivated and caught by the heavenly vision, you will automatically receive the divine commission to go forth and rescue His people from the world with all its temptations and entanglements. If, on the other hand, there is vision but there is no commission attached to it, then you can be sure that the vision is only a mirage such as one sometimes experiences seeing while traveling through the desert. But with every *heavenly* vision there will be the issuance of a divine commission. God never gives a vision for you merely to enjoy. On the contrary, His vision is given with a meaning and purpose behind it. God gives His servant a vision in order that He can commission that one to fulfill that vision. And with the commission there will come forth the servant's vocation.

Now what is a servant of God's vocation? It is not that one be a teacher or a doctor or a nurse or an office worker or an engineer or a housewife or whatever else it might be. Rather, our vocation is to serve God; but if we lack His vision, we have no vocation. In the case of Moses, once he saw that vision of the thorn bush and was thereafter immediately commissioned by God to return to Egypt and rescue His people from bondage to the world, that very commission became Moses' vocation for the rest of his life. It was the one and only task he had to fulfill; and though it was very costly—it costing him everything, Moses had to fulfill his God-given vocation.

Do realize and acknowledge that as God's servants everything concerning us has to be subjected to that vocation: whether family, friends, a career in teaching or in business or in some other profession, one's position in the community, or whatever else it might be. All has to be subordinated to that divinely-commissioned vocation of ours, because our vocation is nothing less than to serve the living God. As a matter of fact, there is no vocation on earth higher than this for God's servants.

And thank God, it is a vocation that can be shared in, participated in, by all believers in the Lord. It is not merely for a few of God's redeemed people to have that vocation. Every Christian, once born again of God's Spirit, is called to be a servant of God, and as such, what becomes his or her lifelong vocation thereafter is simply but preeminently this: to serve the living God and His purpose on earth. Oh, that we may serve Him with all our hearts!

Shall we pray:

> Our heavenly Father, we do bow before Thee; we marvel at Thy mercy. We who should be consumed, and yet, Thou hast glorified us. Oh, that we, low and humble as we are, are called to serve Thee and serve Thy purpose. Our Father, do cause us to forget everything else and just give ourselves completely to Thee and allow Thee to work out that which Thou hast commissioned us to do. We dare not trust in ourselves anymore, but thank God, we can trust Thee. Thou art with us, and the work which thou hast called us to perform shall be done. We pray in the name of our Lord Jesus. Amen.

Chapter Three

The Last Forty Years

Exodus 4:1-9—And Moses answered and said, But behold, they will not believe me, nor hearken unto my voice; for they will say, Jehovah has not appeared to thee. And Jehovah said to him, What is that in thy hand? And he said, A staff [or, a rod]. And he said, Cast it on the ground. And he cast it on the ground, and it became a serpent; and Moses fled from before it. And Jehovah said to Moses, Stretch out thy hand and take it by the tail—and he stretched out his hand and caught it, and it became a staff in his hand—that they may believe that Jehovah, the God of their fathers, the God of Abraham, the God of Isaac, and the God of Jacob, hath appeared unto thee.

And Jehovah said moreover to him, Put now thy hand into thy bosom. And he put his hand into his bosom, and took it out, and behold, his hand was leprous, as snow. And he said, Put thy hand into thy bosom again. And he put his hand into his bosom again, and took it out of his bosom, and behold, it was turned again as his flesh. And it shall come to pass, if they will not believe thee, neither hearken to the voice of the first sign, that they will believe the voice of the other sign. And it shall come to pass, if they will not believe also those two signs, neither hearken unto thy voice, that thou shalt take of the water of the river, and pour it on the dry land; and the water that thou takest out of the river shall become blood upon the dry land.

Numbers 12:3—But the man Moses was very meek, above all men that were upon the face of the earth.

In recent weeks we have been considering together before the Lord the first eighty years in the life of the servant of God, Moses. And today I would like for us to consider the last forty years of his life. We have come to see and understand that the first two forty-year periods were years of preparation for Moses. God had been preparing His servant for eighty years and He then used him during his final forty years as God's now highly useful servant. Why were there so many years spent in preparation for the time when God would finally use him? Just here I would have us pause for a few moments and observe the earthly life of Jesus. God the Father prepared this servant of His—proportionately speaking—during even more years than He did Moses before. God had Jesus undertake just three years' work of service! Hence, for God to spend eighty years in preparing Moses for forty years of service was not something out of the ordinary.

What about us who are God's servants today? Often we are very impatient. We desire to get to the work of ministry immediately, once we have received God's call; but we either ignore or else are ignorant of the fact that God needs to *prepare us first*, otherwise, without some necessary preparation beforehand, He cannot use us because we need to be brought to the point in our lives wherein we shall be serving *Him* and no longer ourselves.

I therefore desire that in our time together today we focus our attention not upon the work which God sent Moses forth to accomplish but upon the man Moses himself as God's servant. Now it must be added that I well realize that God sent Moses forth to do a tremendous work in delivering the children of Israel out of Egypt and through the wilderness in order for them to enter the Promised Land. God also gave Moses the law, and showed him the pattern for the tabernacle as well. Obviously the work which Moses was commissioned to undertake was a monumental task, and it would be most fascinating and most profitable for us to consider that work; but such is not my burden for what we should focus our attention upon in today's fellowship together. Rather, I want us to look closely at Moses himself as the Lord's servant.

Or we could even describe our interest in Moses for today in the following terms: As he was engaged in the work, why was it that God accepted his service? Why was it that God could say, "Moses, My servant"? Again, why was it that Moses' work was readily approved and therefore accepted by God? What, in fact, was the secret of his servanthood? What were the qualifications which he needed to meet? What, in other words, were the things which made Moses a true servant of God? In short, all of the foregoing inquiries is what I would like for us to consider together on this occasion; yet not in any way to slight the work of Moses, for he indeed accomplished a tremendous set of tasks. Nevertheless, in our time together today on the life of Moses, I would like our interest to be centered more upon the worker himself than on his work.

Now I believe that during Moses' last forty years on earth when he was serving God and serving the children of Israel, there were two characteristics which marked the way he conducted himself which clearly stand out as evidence that Moses was a true servant of God. And the first of these which I want us to consider revolves around the matter of authority and meekness—that is to say, the manner in which Moses exercised spiritual authority among God's people of that day as balanced throughout by his spirit of meekness.

We see authority in Moses on the one hand and meekness on the other. No one can do any spiritual work without exercising authority. Spiritual authority is a must, and surely Moses was a man of authority; and this authority was represented by the rod in his hand. We cannot separate God's servant Moses from his rod or staff; for that was the symbol of his authority.

Now we often view a person who wields authority as being one who is harsh and severe in demeanor—one who is strong in conduct to the point of manifesting only hardness and insensitivity. In the case of Moses, in fact, artists and sculptors have generally depicted him as a man of tremendous strength and energy, and whose masculinity is of a kind projecting the notion of despotism and tyrannical authority coming forth from him. That, however, is not an accurate picture of Moses, according to the Scriptures. It is quite true, of course, that he was a man of great authority, but the Bible also declares that he was the meekest of all men on earth.

Naturally speaking, we might think these two characteristics—authority and meekness—are contradictory to each other. If you are a person with authority you may perhaps think you have to appear very strong, that perhaps you think you must step on everybody; and that if you are a meek person, then you become, will-nilly, the doormat for everybody to step on *you*. Such thoughts as these will quite naturally cause a person to view these two traits as contradictory. But we need to realize that spiritual authority and true meekness must go together, thus balancing each other out: if there is spiritual authority present, it should be exercised in the spirit of meekness; and if there is true meekness present, there is bound to be tremendous strength manifested. And this is what we find in the conduct and demeanor of Moses as God's true servant.

Moses saw the thorn-bush vision; he heard and received the divine commission; but he was then moved to say the following to Jehovah God: "It is true, I have seen You, and I have heard You. You are sending me back to Egypt to deliver the children of Israel, but if I go back, they will not believe me. They will say, 'God has not appeared to you.' How, then, can I convince the children of Israel that You have indeed appeared to me and have sent me. What I need from You, oh God, are some credentials which I can present to Your people." To rephrase Moses' response to God's commission in New Testament terms, here is what God's servant was saying: "What are the signs of my apostleship? How will people know that I have been sent by God? How can I prove to them that it is God who has sent me?"

Obviously, that was an important matter to be considered. So here was the interplay which occurred between Master and servant: God said to Moses, "What is in your hand?" And Moses replied, "A shepherd's staff, a shepherd's rod." God instructed His servant, "Throw it to the ground." And as Moses threw the rod down, it turned into a serpent, and Moses immediately fled from it. Then God said, "Stretch out your hand and pick it up by the tail." So Moses stretched out his hand and took it up by the tail, and it once again became a rod in his hand. God then observed: "The voice of this rod will be heard; the people will believe you."

God next said to His servant: "Yet, if they do not believe you by means of the voice of this sign, then I will give you another one: Put your hand into your bosom." So Moses put his hand into his bosom, and when he drew it out it was leprous. God said, "Put your hand back onto your bosom again." So he put his hand back again next to his bosom and drew it out, and his hand became as fresh as it had been before.

God then explained, as follows: "If the people do not listen to the voice of the first sign, they will listen to the voice of this second sign. Even so, if they do not listen to the voice of these two signs, then I will provide you with yet another one. You are to collect some water from the river Nile and pour it upon the dry ground, and it will turn into blood, and surely they will now believe you." These, then, became the signs of Moses' apostleship which he took with him back into Egypt. By these signs the Israelites could realize that he was truly sent by God; and in a sense all of us who would be God's servants today need such credentials.

What, therefore, does a rod represent? A rod or staff in Scripture speaks of power, authority, rule, dominion, even strength like steel. For instance, we read in Psalm 110 that "Jehovah shall send the scepter [or, rod] of thy might out of Zion: [therefore,] rule in the midst of thine enemies" (v.2). Again, Revelation 19 declares that the Lord "shall rule the nations with an iron rod" (see v. 15b ASV). Hence, with regard to Moses, a shepherd's rod in his hand was representative of the fact of his rule, authority, strength and power over his sheep. And it needs to be noticed that it was by this rod that Moses made his living; he depended on this rod for his very livelihood. Such, then, was the meaning and significance of Moses' rod.

Do realize that each one of us has a rod: each one of us has some kind of authority, power, or strength like steel by which we live: whatever natural gifts, talents, educational attainment and/or experience we may possess—all such, as it were, becomes a rod in our hand, and it is by this rod that we make our living; moreover, we depend upon the content of this rod to do whatever work God may have given us to do. We each may not be a shepherd; instead, each of us may be a doctor, a nurse, a teacher, or a housewife; nevertheless, each child of God has a rod in his or her hand. Each one of us has a rod of which to boast and upon which to lean. Each of God's children has that which to employ in order to maintain his or her position in society and to fulfill his or her career work. Such, then, is our rod.

However, should that rod leave our hand and touch the earth it shall become like to a serpent—that which can hurt or harm people. We know, of course, that a serpent in the Scriptures always speaks of Satan and/or satanic power. In other words, that which we have, depend on, even boast about—that which makes us what we are and enables us to do what in life we are supposed to do—if it touches the earth it will become serpent-like in nature.

Whatever talents you may have—whatever skill, power, authority, and/or strength you may possess, if it should touch the fallen earth and come under the grasp and control of the enemy, Satan, he will turn it into something harmful to the world. Satan is the ancient serpent, and he will take hold, if he can, of the talents, power, authority, or skill of man and use such rods to hurt and harm people.

That, in fact, is what we may possibly find today among those who would be God's servants. Some of God's people may think that they hold their rod in their own hand. Yet, they do not realize that their rod has already left them and has already touched the fallen earth. Oh, how Satan makes use of human power, authority, wisdom, strength, energy and/or skill, and turns such rods into that which is hurtful and harmful. And that is what we are experiencing in not only the unbelieving world today but even also among God's people who would be His servants. The cleverest mind and the most talented among us can be used by Satan to do the worst damage to the people of this world and even to those among the body of Christ.

Now God's servant Moses fled from his rod-turned-serpent. He realized that if the rod he had could be taken hold of by Satan, it would be quite dangerous to others; and hence, he had to flee. Do we, like Moses, realize this? Do we not understand that if Satan should get hold of our particular rod and we do not realize it because we think we are still holding and controlling it in our own hand, then it is out of our hand already. It is one of the most dangerous situations in the world and we therefore need, like Moses, to flee from it immediately. Are you afraid of your talent-rod becoming a serpent? Are you fearful that your skill-rod could become a tool of the enemy? Are you fearful that your strength-rod could turn into a serpent? Are you afraid that your power-rod could be used by some Satanic power? Are you afraid that your rod of authority could turn into a serpent? Oh, if you are not fearful of this happening, then I am afraid for you.

Let us all flee from such a possibility which can do much damage, hurt and harm.

Let us notice again that God said to Moses: "Stretch out your hand and take the snake by its tail." Now I do not know how true it is, but I have been told that if you hold a snake up by its tail and shake it, that snake will die. And by Moses doing so, that rod-turned-into-a-snake became once more a rod in Moses' hand; but we must clearly understand that this rod now became *God's* rod. In other words, it was no longer the original shepherd's rod which had been held previously in Moses' hand: it was no longer the rod which had become a serpent; on the contrary, it was now God's rod. How did it become God's rod? Let us see that Moses' original shepherd's rod had gone through an upside-down and downside-up process; which is to say, that Moses' rod had gone through the process of death and resurrection. And once having gone through such a process, Moses' rod became the rod of God.

From this we can conclude that whatever talent, whatever energy, whatever strength, whatever position, whatever authority, whatever power, whatever education, whatever experience God in His providence has given you, if such remains in *your* hand, it can only help you make a living. Furthermore, if any of these rods should leave your hand and touch the fallen earth, the enemy will grasp hold of it and thus it will become the most dangerous instrument of harm and hurt in the whole world. If, though, you are willing to let your rod go through death and resurrection and thus become an instrument in *God's* hand, such shall become the rod of God wielded by the hand of His servant, and which shall serve as the symbol of that servant's spiritual authority. It was by exercising this authority that Moses was able to fulfill the work which God had commissioned him to do.

God had said to His servant Moses: "Take this rod of Mine with you when you go back to Egypt." In line with this statement, therefore, we learn by reading the books of Exodus and Numbers that whenever a miracle was performed by the hand of Moses—and whether done for the purpose of punishing the enemy or for the sake of delivering the children of Israel—it was through the instrumentality of this very rod by which the miracle was accomplished. For whenever Moses stretched forth the rod of God, something quite extraordinary happened. For instance, Moses smote the Red Sea with God's rod and its waters parted to the left and right. Every miraculous action taken was by means of this very rod, which thus was the manifestation of Moses' authority in doing God's work.

If we want to serve God, we must have and assert His rod; on the contrary, we must never assert an untransformed shepherd's rod or a rod which, having touched the fallen earth, becomes a serpent. Are we willing to let the particular rod or rods we have, which we deem to be the source of our power and authority, go into death? If so, then we shall discover that through the process of that death unto resurrection God can use these transformed rods of ours to perform the work which He has called us to do. Such will therefore become the symbol of spiritual authority, and that is what we each must have if we would be true servants of God. Let that rod of talent, gift, ability, strength, or experience which you have go through the death-and-resurrection process and be placed in God's hand, and He will use that transformed rod of yours for His glory.

Now if God's people do not believe the voice of that first sign, there is made available the voice of a second sign. God therefore instructed Moses to do the following: "Put your hand into your bosom." Moses did so, but when he removed his hand it was leprous. Let us look at our hands. We may think they are clean, but place one of them upon our heart and pull it away, and what do we discover? We discover that like that hand of ours, our heart is leprous. Oh! We read in Jeremiah 17 that our heart is deceitful above all things and exceedingly corrupt: who can plumb its depths of deceit and corruption? But God can, and does (see v. 9). The problem, of course, lies not in our hand; the problem lies in our heart. And so, what is the condition of our heart? It is nothing less than leprous.

Leprosy in the Old and New Testaments represent sin. Sin is like leprosy. A leper may have leprosy in him or her, but it can lie dormant for twenty or thirty years. Nobody knows it; but then it can break out everywhere. It can break out on the top of one's head, on one's feet, or upon any other part of a person's body. In the olden days leprosy was considered incurable. The leper was unclean and had to live outside of the people's camp. Moreover, when people came near the leper, that one had to place a covering upon the beard and shout out: "Unclean, unclean! Stay away from me!" (see Leviticus 13:45-46) That is a picture of sin. We who have sinned are like lepers and are unclean before God. That is what we are.

So God showed Moses what he himself was, and in so many words He was saying to him: "By putting your hand into your bosom and pulling it away it became leprous; for that is what you in yourself are. You are like a leper, unclean. Consider that fact, Moses: How can an unclean hand handle My rod?" But then, God said to Moses: "Put your hand back upon your heart again." He put his hand back and then drew it out, and his flesh was as fresh as ever.

This second sign which God showed His servant is reflective of one of the great themes or principles to be found in God's word, and it is known as the principle of the second or the principle of grace. Whereas law is the subject of the first principle, grace is that of the second. So here in this instance with Moses we have demonstrated for us the principle of the second which is grace—wherein God, in so many words, is found saying to Moses: "You are as leprous in My sight as would be a leper, but I in My grace cleanse you and sanctify you, and with this hand of yours you can now hold and use My rod."

Let us see that a rod represents power whereas a hand represents life. God's servant needs a pure life if he or she is to handle the power and authority of God. Those two things—rod and hands—must therefore go into death. Some people have great power, but they do not have a corresponding life with which to exercise that power in order to help others. In other words, if a person is given power and authority and that person's hands are unclean, they hurt rather than help. So, we need an appropriate life with which to back up our power. The spiritual power or authority which God has given us has to be wielded or exercised by the divine life of Christ in us. It is not God's will that the flesh should exercise any of His authority; on the contrary, it must be the Holy Spirit of life in us who is to exercise spiritual authority. Hence, the voice of the second sign has reference to the life of God. If we have God's life, people will see it and will listen to it.

Thus, these two signs are the key credentials of every true servant of the Lord. On the one hand, God's servant must have a rod; on the other hand, God's servant must have proper hands. The rod represents the spiritual authority of God; the hand represents the spiritual life of God. And these two spiritual realities must be combined together as the signs of apostleship. Yet, let us understand that concerning these two signs, it is a matter of degree, not of kind. Yes, every one of God's servants must have these two signs if he or she wants to serve God, but from person to person there will naturally be different degrees possessed of these two signs.

Now if the Israelites—and for that matter, the Egyptians—do not hear and accept these two signs given by God to His servant Moses, what then? God gave a third sign. He instructed His servant that upon his return to Egypt he was to draw water out of the Nile River, pour it on the dry ground, and it would turn into blood. The river Nile was the life stream of Egypt. The Egyptians drank from that river, they planted crops along the side of that river; in short, it was their very life source. If, however, they were to reject the authority of God, if they were to reject the grace of God, what would happen? Judgment! And that is a most serious issue.

We know, of course, that a lot of authority is marked by human substitutes; but if the authority really comes from God, if a person has truly been sent by God, if there is a life that can prove and back up the authority being exercised, then whoever does not listen to that one is in reality also not listening to God himself, and the result shall be judgment. So the first result will be judgment. If people do not listen to God's servant, there will be judgment. And so, it was with authority such as this that Moses returned to Egypt to lead the children out from there and on through the wilderness in order to bring them into the Promised Land.

Nevertheless, authority is but one of those two key credentials of apostolic servanthood. That credential has to be balanced with the other key credential: meekness. If authority is not combined with meekness it can do great harm. Be advised here that Moses was as firm as a rock whenever his wielding of authority was related to God—to His truth, will and desired undertakings. In this regard, therefore, Moses would never compromise, for he represented God and His truth, will, and authority. And because of this, Moses could not and would not ever compromise. In other words, Moses would never lower God's standard of truth and righteousness. He had to stand with God in all things, and in that sense he was most firm, very strong. He would not yield an inch, and thank God for that!

Please note, however, that this authority which Moses exercised did not make him hard, cold, harsh, dictatorial, or tyrannical. On the other hand, we shall soon learn in some detail that whenever an issue arose which pertained to himself personally, Moses never defended himself. Authority, though, is related to God and to the things of God, and because of that reality there can be no negotiation nor compromise. If a servant of God is willing to compromise God's truth, will and way, that person is no longer God's servant and thus forfeits the authority God had given.

Accordingly, whenever you speak for God, you as His servant must speak with authority because you are representing God; it is not you yourself speaking. You therefore cannot ever lower God's standard; you cannot ever compromise. No matter if people should say, as did those who said to the Lord Jesus himself, "This is a hard saying; who can hear it?" (John 6:60), you, as the representative of God, must react, as did Jesus, by not lowering or diluting the divine standard one iota to suit or satisfy people's wish or taste. You, like the Lord Jesus, cannot do that because the authority you wield is related to God and to the spiritual well-being of His children.

However, whenever an issue arises which touches upon the servant himself, that situation is a different matter. Let us remind ourselves that though the Scriptures describe Moses as being later most meek and tender, he was not like that before. Let us recall that he was brought up and reared in the Egyptian palace to be a prince. He was taught and trained to be proud, self-confident, commanding, lording it over all those around him who were of a lower social class. And when he eventually launched forth on his own, that was how he conducted himself; but that behavior proved entirely ineffective. However, while Moses was in the wilderness for forty years, God trained him in the spirit of meekness. This we can correctly conclude from the well-known fact that no one can shepherd sheep whose treatment towards them is that of aloofness, arrogance, harshness, or uncaring handling. On the contrary, a shepherd must take care of sheep tenderly, softly, compassionately, and with great sensitivity. And thus, Moses learned from God to exercise the spirit of meekness towards people just as he had learned what shepherding sheep required of him as a shepherd.

Now how do we know that in his day Moses was the meekest person above all people on the earth? Recall that Moses had a sister, Miriam, and a brother, Aaron. Actually, Miriam was an older sibling who really took good care of her little baby brother. For when Moses had been placed inside that ark in the river Nile, it was Miriam who was ever present watching among the reeds (Exodus 2:1-7). So Miriam had a great interest in Moses.

Miriam was also a prophetess. We will remember that after the Israelites had crossed the Red Sea, it was Miriam who had led the women in singing the song of victory (Exodus 15:20-21). And Aaron, who was the older brother of Moses, was the high priest. God did reveal himself to both Miriam and Aaron, but for some reason, when they were in the wilderness (Numbers 12) they became jealous of Moses.

These three were the leaders of the children of Israel. Moses, of course, was *the* leader, Aaron was the high priest, and Miriam was the prophetess; but we learn from the Biblical record that there surfaced a jealousy in the two older siblings towards the youngest among these three. And if we delve deeper into the narrative, we discover that it most likely arose over Miriam's competition with Moses' wife Zipporah. Miriam had wanted to oversee Moses because over the many years she had become so attached to him. But, of course, Moses and Zipporah, as husband and wife, had a close marriage relationship. But because of Miriam's jealousy towards Zipporah, she began to say falsely that Moses had married a Cushite woman (Numbers 12:1). This accusation Miriam could say about Zipporah because probably she was a little dark of skin and thus she was really looked down upon by Moses' sister. It was pure jealousy—a woman's jealousy.

These two siblings were interested in obtaining Moses' love, and out of that circumstance Miriam began inappropriately to influence her brother Aaron. I do not think Aaron was so much concerned about Moses' wife, but certainly he was concerned about Moses' position of leadership. Hence, that is probably the reason why all these developments came about; and so, these two older siblings began to criticize Moses:

"Did God speak to you alone, Moses? Has not God spoken to us, too? Why should you be the topmost leader?" Most surely God *had* spoken to them. But when Moses heard these accusatory words, did he say or do anything? Did he attempt to defend himself? Not in the least. Moses heard these harsh words, but he said nothing and did nothing. He accepted the criticism with meekness. Now that is a manifestation of humble meekness. If an issue concerned God, Moses as God's servant would not yield an inch, but if the issue concerned himself he would say nothing. And the result was that God spoke on Moses' behalf.

Please realize that if you say too much, God will not speak for you. It is better that you not say anything and simply let God speak; not as a matter of policy but of truth. The sister and the brother criticized Moses without any justification; indeed, they exaggerated. On the other hand, Moses would not explain himself nor did he defend himself; he just received their word in silence. And that is the strength of meekness because by this time Moses thought nothing of himself.

Let us now observe God's reaction. He called these three together to the entrance to the tent of meeting and spoke to them. Said God to these three: "Indeed, I speak to a prophet, but I speak to that one by dreams and visions. It is not so with My servant Moses. I speak with him face to face. How dare you two criticize my servant!" And God withdrew from them in a wrath; but after he left, Aaron noticed that Miriam had become leprous! So Aaron pleaded with Moses, and Moses in turn pleaded with God. He asked Him to heal Miriam, and God heard him. Now that is the result of meekness.

During this entire forty-year period of leading the Israelites to Canaan Moses maintained a very interesting—even extraordinary—posture. Whenever people began to murmur against him, criticize him, or attack him personally, what was Moses' reaction? Moses fell upon his face on each occasion. Now if someone criticizes you or verbally attacks you, how will you react? Naturally speaking, would you not stand high up and assert yourself? Indeed, that is the way most people would react. However, every time the people criticized or said anything against Moses, he would fall down upon his face. Yet it was not only that he did so before God; the Bible tells us that he also fell upon his face before the people. Do consider this, if you will: that if, in the face of personal criticism or of being spoken against unjustly, you assume the posture—as did Moses—of being the lowest, or assume the attitude of being the worst, what in the end can those critics and murmurers do to you any further? Since in their minds they have now reduced you to zero, what more can they do to you? Nothing more.

Numbers chapters 1-10 tell us of the preparation for the movement towards the Promised Land, and in chapter 11 we learn that the children of Israel began to move from Mount Sinai. And as soon as they moved from there something unpleasant happened. This was due to the fact that the multitude of people who had been delivered out of Egypt were not all Israelites but were actually to some extent a mixed multitude (11:4a). This had come about because these non-Jews—who constituted a small minority among the children of Israel—had been attracted by the power of God and had therefore exited Egypt with the Israelites. As a result, this minority ended up causing problems.

For instance, at this point in the people's move away from Mount Sinai, these non-Jews began to complain, and declared: "We are tired of this manna. Every day we eat this manna and nothing else. We remember what we had to eat back in Egypt: all those delicious smelly things like fish, leeks, garlic, melons, cucumbers, and onions. But now, this manna is so flat in taste that we are tired of eating it." Unfortunately, this murmuring began to spread throughout the entire camp. So much so that all the children of Israel themselves began to murmur as well (11:4-6). When Moses heard it, he could not stand it anymore. So he went before God and said, "Why did You assign me the task of taking care of these children like a mother or a father?

The responsibility is just too much for me to handle; I had rather die, for I do not wish to see these people cry. It is just too much for me" (see 11:10-15).

So God said to Moses in response: "All right, if it is too much for you, call together seventy elders from among the children of Israel and I will take a portion of the Spirit from you and give to these seventy people so that they can bear the responsibility with you." Here we can observe how gracious God is. He did not say, "Call the seventy together and I will give them the Spirit." No, He instead said, "I will take a portion of the Spirit that is upon you and put on them, and thus you shall not bear the burden alone." In so many words God was explaining the following: Don't you know, Moses, that the Spirit on you is enough for this task? If, however, you think it is too much for you to handle alone, all right, I will let these seventy share the Spirit with the people. These seventy will therefore take responsibility together with you; but you must realize that this entire responsibility is going to be accomplished by the Spirit and not by you or by the seventy" (see 11:16-17, 24-25).

So Moses called the seventy together, but two of them did not want to be a part of the seventy. They too must have been among those who were against Moses. They were two of the leaders, Eldad and Medad, and they did not even bother to come when Moses summoned the seventy. They instead remained in the camp; even so, the Spirit fell on them anyway. So these two began to prophesy in the camp, and very soon some young men ran up to Moses and reported: "Those two men—Eldad and Medad—are prophesying in the camp!" And Joshua, one among these young men and who was also Moses' aide, being jealous for the well-being of Moses, advised his master: "Lord, forbid them." But Moses responded with these selfless words: "Oh, no, do not say that. Would that *all* God's people would become prophets" (11:26-29). That is an expression of meekness and an indication of non-self-interest or -concern.

In Numbers chapters 13 and 14 we are told that when the ten spies returned to the Israelite camp and reported negatively of what they saw in the Promised Land, the people began to howl and cry out, they accusing Moses as follows: "Why did you bring us here? We would rather die back in Egypt or even back in the wilderness, for now we are going to be killed by the Canaanites who will then take our children and our wives; therefore, let us appoint among ourselves another leader to lead us back." And Moses immediately reacted by once more falling upon his face before the people (13:25-14:5). On this occasion we see again that Moses never spoke for himself; he accepted in silence the criticism which came his way and left it with God to vindicate him. That was an expression of meekness in this servant of God once more.

Furthermore, we learn from Numbers chapter 16 that the rebel, Korah, and his company of two hundred and fifty leaders of the children of Israel rebelled against Moses and Aaron and harshly criticized them. Korah accused them, declaring: "The whole congregation is holy; why do you lift yourselves up as though you are holier than anybody else?" Moses and Aaron had never once done that; nevertheless, Korah and his fellow rebels accused them of having done such. Once again Moses fell down upon his face before everyone, for that was his posture continually. Every time he was criticized, down he went. That is true meekness.

Moreover, when God told Moses to inform the people what the punishment for these rebels would be, Moses in meekness said the following: "This is not what I want to do; nevertheless, it is necessary in order to show that this is from God." Whereupon the earth instantly opened up and swallowed alive into Hades Korah and all the company of rebels.

Even so, the Israelites further rebelled, for they now ridiculously accused Moses of having done this himself, with the result that God caused a plague to descend and spread upon the people. Immediately Moses, knowing the way of the Lord, instructed Aaron to take vessels of incense quickly and stand between the living and the dead, and thus Moses saved the day for most of the children of Israel.

It was always in the spirit of meekness that Moses served God and served His people. And that was the reason God could earnestly and proudly say, "Moses, My servant." For he was different.

If we want to serve God we must indeed have authority, but let us never forget that the authority we are to exercise is not natural authority. That spiritual authority has to come forth through the process of death and resurrection. It has to be wielded by that person whose life is of God. And there must also be the spirit of meekness in the exercising of that authority. Paul the apostle-servant of God wrote in I Corinthians 4: "Do you Corinthian believers want me to come with a rod or come to you in a spirit of meekness?" (see v.21) Let us also recall what the Lord Jesus himself once said: "Take My yoke upon you and learn of Me, for I am lowly and meek of heart; and you shall have rest in your soul" (see Matthew 11:29).

May the Lord therefore help us all as servants of God to serve Him acceptably. And ever bear in mind that we need both authority *and* meekness if we would serve God aright.

Shall we pray:

> Our heavenly Father, how we praise and thank Thee that Thou hast called us to serve Thee in Thy work. Every one of us is called. We do pray that we may not be those who are called but not chosen. We pray instead that we may all be chosen because we ourselves do choose Thee as our Master, as our Lord. Oh God, we pray that Thou wouldst teach us how to serve Thee. Grant us the authority that is from above. Give us a life that can back up the authority which Thou hast given; and also, oh God, do develop in us a spirit of meekness. We pray that

we may stand as a lion whenever Thy truth, will, or purpose are involved; but that we may be meek as a lamb whenever an issue involves ourselves personally—because that is what Thou art in Thy character. We ask in the name of our Lord Jesus. Amen.

Chapter Four

Faith and Faithfulness

Hebrews 11:24-29—By faith Moses, when he had become great [that is, matured in age], refused to be called son of Pharaoh's daughter; choosing rather to suffer affliction along with the people of God than to have the temporary pleasure of sin; esteeming the reproach of the Christ greater riches than the treasures of Egypt, for he had respect to the recompense. By faith he left Egypt, not fearing the wrath of the king; for he persevered, as seeing him who is invisible. By faith he celebrated the Passover and the sprinkling of the blood, that the destroyer of the firstborn might not touch them.

By faith they passed through the Red sea as through dry land; of which the Egyptians having made trial were swallowed up.

Hebrews 3:5—And Moses indeed was faithful in all his house, as a ministering servant, for a testimony of the things to be spoken after.

We have been considering together Moses as God's servant. Moses was called by God to be His servant, to serve His purpose in his time. In like manner, we too are called to be God's servants, and to serve Him and His purpose in our generation (cf. Acts 13:36a NIV, NASB). And just as Moses was chosen by God so we too have been chosen—chosen even before the foundation of the world, set apart even in our mother's womb, and called by His grace (Galatians 1:15). Moreover, having been chosen by God, one day Moses was himself moved to choose God. In fact, when he was forty years old, he chose to suffer with the people of God rather than enjoy all the pleasures of Egypt. Likewise, there comes a day when we, too, who have been chosen by God, must make a choice: shall we choose God more than anything or anyone else? Shall we have Him rather than have anything else in the world?

Furthermore, God not only chose Moses, He also trained him. As we saw earlier, Moses had to learn, unlearn, and learn many things, and that must be the same experience which will be necessary for us to have. For instance, there are many things in our past which we have learned and, having learned them, we think we can depend upon them; but God has made clear through Moses' experience that we have to unlearn them; and then we will need to learn many new things concerning our God. Only through such a process as that can we become usable in God's hands.

Hence, in serving God there are a few things which are absolutely necessary for us to learn concerning God and His way and purpose. One such was what was mentioned last time: the matter of authority and meekness. We saw that Moses served God with authority, yet not the authority which comes from man but from God. It was authority according to the life of God and the gift of God. In addition, we came to see that such authority must be exercised with meekness; and because Moses had learned this lesson so well, God was moved to describe him as the meekest of all men. Thus, he was able to serve God's purpose. Accordingly, we too need to learn what spiritual authority is and how it must be wielded: true spiritual authority is not a matter of position but a matter of life, and it needs to be exercised with meekness—we not thinking of ourselves but only of God.

Now today we will conclude our discussion of Moses by considering another matter which is absolutely essential if we want to serve God well, and that is the twin issues of faith and faithfulness. Moses served God with faith and he served God with faithfulness. We are informed in Hebrews 11 that without faith it is impossible for anyone to please God, for we are further told there that whoever would come to God must believe that He is—that He exists, and that He is the Rewarder of those who seek after Him (v. 6). If we do not have faith, there cannot even be a beginning to our spiritual life. In the case of Moses, it was by faith that his parents hid him for three months, and it was by faith that when Moses was forty years old, he refused to be called any longer the son of Pharaoh's daughter; rather, he chose the reproach of Christ and the forfeit of all the riches of Egypt because he considered the far more worthy recompense which would await him. It was by faith that Moses became later what he was.

There is another verse about Moses in Hebrews 11 which explains that, "by faith he left Egypt, not fearing the wrath of the king; for he persevered, as seeing him who is invisible" (v. 27). On the other hand, two verses in Exodus 2 read: "Then Moses feared, and said, Surely the matter of my murder of the Egyptian is known." In fact, "Pharaoh heard of this matter, and sought to slay Moses. But Moses fled from before Pharaoh" (vv. 14c-15a, b). Now according to the record of Exodus, when Moses heard that the news had gotten out that he had killed an Egyptian, he was afraid because he was certain that the matter was known—presumably known not only to the Israelites but to Pharaoh as well, and for that reason he fled. Yet the author of Hebrews, inspired by the Holy Spirit, comments on that incident by saying, "By faith he left Egypt." Exodus would indicate that Moses fled Egypt out of fear, but here in Hebrews we are told that Moses left Egypt, not fearing Pharaoh's wrath. Whereas Exodus states that Moses heard that the matter was known (to the king) and so he feared and fled for his life, Hebrews asserts that he did not fear the wrath of the king and left the country. Now is there any contradiction?

It is quite true that in the Bible sometimes the Old Testament will present the history of an event and the New Testament will offer up a comment which may not seem to agree with the history. And yet as Christians we know and believe that both must be true. So how, in this case, are we going to reconcile the historical record with the Holy Spirit's judgment upon that record? Admittedly, this verse has been a real difficulty for many commentators, and quite naturally, there are at least two different interpretations.

The first is this: if both the Exodus and Hebrew verses refer to the incident when Moses fled after he killed the Egyptian, then the explanation is true that he was afraid when he heard the news had spread, and so, assuming that the king knew about it, he fled the country. But further, according to this interpretation, at the same time Moses was a man of faith; and hence, the reason he left Egypt rather than give himself up to Pharaoh was because he believed that God still had His hand upon him, and that he would therefore not expose himself to Pharaoh by casting himself upon the king's mercy, and thus give up the work to which God had called him; instead of doing that, Moses persevered in carrying out the work because he saw the Invisible One. Now that is one interpretation, which assumes that both the Exodus and Hebrew texts refer to the same event.

However, another interpretation claims that the Scripture portion in Hebrews does not refer to Moses fleeing from Egypt following his murder of the Egyptian; rather, it refers to the time when—forty years later—he led the children of Israel out of Egypt. We are told elsewhere in the book of Exodus that on the occasion when Moses for the last time came before Pharaoh, he warned the king that if he would not let the people go, something terrible would happen: God's destroying angel would come and kill all the firstborn of Egypt. Pharaoh did not believe this warning and—out of anger towards Moses—he had declared: "Get thee from me, take heed to thyself, see my face no more; for in the day thou seest my face thou shalt die" (10:28). Here Moses was not intimidated at all by Pharaoh, but he went out not fearing the anger of the king. Instead, he persevered in God's work by leading the children of Israel out of Egypt, having by faith seen Him who is invisible.

This second interpretation is quite possible if we notice the different verb tenses used in these verses. According to the historical chronology, of course, Moses had fled Egypt first following his murder of the Egyptian, and then, four decades later, he had led the children of Israel out of Egypt immediately following the inaugural Passover feast. In other words, after observing the Passover event, Moses left Egypt. So it would seem that Hebrews 11:27 should refer to his departure from Egypt leading forth the Israelites, since verse 28 mentions the Passover and, in the original Greek text, uses the present participle—"has celebrated."* So advocates of this interpretation believe that because of the difference in verb tenses, Hebrews 11:27 must refer to the exodus of God's people out of Egypt under Moses' leadership.

Nevertheless, whatever may be the correct view, I think both verses in Exodus and Hebrews illustrate one very important feature: faith is absolutely necessary for our spiritual life. If we want to experience spiritual life we must have faith. Without faith Moses would not have been hid for three months; he would have died. Without faith Moses would not have chosen the reproach of Christ. Without faith he would not have been able to withstand the wrath of Pharaoh and persevere to the very end. With respect to spiritual life, therefore, we need faith throughout, and I believe we all readily understand that.

---

* Among all English translations of the Bible or New Testament (59 in all), the only translation of Hebrews 11:28 which adheres to the original Greek verb tense is that to be found in *The Disciples' Literal New Testament: Serving Modern Disciples by More Fully Reflecting the Writing Style of the Ancient Disciples* (DLNT), copyright © 2011 Michael J. Magill, published by Reyma Publishing. DLNT's translation of Hebrews 11:27-28 is as follows:

By faith he left Egypt, not having feared the fury of the king. For he persevered as seeing the invisible One.

By faith he has performed [or, has celebrated] the Passover and the sprinkling *of* the blood in order that the *one* destroying the firstborns might not touch them.—*The Publishers*

However, there is another aspect to this matter under discussion, and that is spiritual work. If we want to do God's spiritual work, it has to be accomplished by faith; otherwise, no truly spiritual work can be pursued. Any work undertaken without the exercise of faith is not God's spiritual work. By faith Moses celebrated the Passover. By faith Moses led the people out of Egypt. By faith Moses led God's people across the Red Sea. From all this we come to understand that the work of God likewise has to be done by faith. Without faith no spiritual work can be accomplished.

Let us consider, for instance, the celebration of Passover. Moses went before Pharaoh and told him: "God said, Let My people go. If not, all the firstborn throughout will be killed." And then God told Moses to tell the children of Israel to prepare a lamb for each house and on that night every family was to kill that lamb and put its blood upon that home's doorposts and lintel. The whole family would be gathered inside the house feasting upon the lamb. And on that same night the Destroyer would pass through all the land of Egypt and if he saw no blood on the entrance door of any home, he would shed the blood of the firstborn within that house. Moses informed both the children of Israel and Pharaoh of all this.

Now how did Moses know this would happen? Never in history had anything like this ever occurred. There was no precedent on which Moses could rely for inspiring confidence. It was going to be the first time ever, there being no previous example for him on which to pin his faith. Nevertheless, because God had said so, Moses believed what He said. Hence, it was by faith that he celebrated Passover. If he had not had faith, would Moses have believed that an angel of destruction would appear and destroy all the firstborn of an entire empire? If he had not had faith, would he have believed that the blood of a lamb could deliver the children of Israel? Of course, to the worldly people it was absurd to even imagine such a thing. How could the blood of a lamb serve as the substitute for the blood of a firstborn child? So it was by faith that Moses instituted that first Passover. It was a work of faith—pure and simple.

Be it understood here that forty years previously Moses had started to work *for* God. When he was forty years old, it came into his mind to go out and see how his brethren fared. So he went out, thinking that he was serving God. He thought he was working for God, and he was, but he it was who took the initiative. It was therefore not a work of faith at all, for he had not waited upon God for *His* timing; indeed, Moses had not in the least been sent by God at that particular moment. He did not consult God as to when and how to do His work, and hence he took upon himself the work for God by going forth himself on his own, laboring by his own wisdom, by his own strength, by his own eloquence, and by his own physical prowess. In short, Moses was working *for* God but not working *with* God.

Let us recognize that there is a great difference between working for God and working with God. The former is doing your own work, but the latter is doing God's work. Outwardly, it may seem to possess the same character; but when you delve into the *source* of the work, you will discern a great difference. Working *for* God is founded upon your initiative; working *with* God means that the work originates with God himself. Undertaking a work for God is doing work by means of your own wisdom and strength, but pursuing a work with God is accomplished through His wisdom, power and strength. Working for God is doing so for your glory, but working with God is laboring for His glory. Working for God does not require faith because you yourself are able to do it, but working with God requires faith in God. Hence, without faith nothing can be done. We see here, then, that there was a great difference between the timings of Moses' service towards God.

Forty years earlier in Moses' life it was a working for God, but forty years later it was a working with God because now He had sent him. Recall that at this moment when he was eighty years old, Moses thought it was the end of his earthly existence, yet God at that very moment said, "Go." In his response Moses said, "How in the world can I possibly go and do what You, oh God, are instructing me to do, for I am too old and nearing the end? How, then, can I possibly deliver the children of Israel? I'm finished; it's impossible; I cannot do it." But God countered with these reassuring words: "I am with you and will go with you. It is not a matter of what *you* can do; it is what I myself am going to do *through* you."

Please be advised that God's work can only be done by God himself. You cannot do it; I cannot do it; Moses could not do it; Paul could not do it; in fact, no one can do it. God's work can only be done by God himself; but He will do it through you, through me, through Moses, through Paul, through whoever relies upon God to do the work.

Moses, by faith, did the work all through the final forty years of his life: from his concluding time in Egypt, then through the wilderness, and up to that concluding moment when the children of Israel finally arrived at the eastern side of the river Jordan. During those forty years all the works which Moses did were accomplished by faith—faith in God and not in himself. We can see very clearly, can we not, that it was not Moses; it was entirely God.

Yes, sometimes Moses was puzzled; sometimes he was frustrated; at times he was even on the verge of giving up, and he would say, "Now why? Why? I just cannot work anymore. Why did You send me, oh God? I have made a fool of myself." Yet, it was not Moses but God who did the work throughout. It was God in Moses who undertook all the work, and because of this, by faith all the work was accomplished.

In the whole history of Moses' service towards God there was one very significant occasion when Moses seemed to lose faith, and that is recorded in Numbers 20. The children of Israel had arrived at the wilderness of Zin, and at that time there was no water. So the people murmured and complained and began to accuse Moses: "Moses, you have led us here, and now you are going to let us die in the wilderness! It would have been much better had we died back in Egypt. We have no water to drink. Why have you done this to us?" And at that moment Moses fell upon his face before the Lord and the people as he usually did.

So the Lord instructed His servant as follows: "Moses, get up; take the staff which is in the tabernacle before My presence, and take it with you to the rock. Gather the people together, speak to the rock in their presence, and water will come forth." Moses got up; he then took the staff from before the ark in the tent of meeting, and gathered the people before the rock; but instead of *speaking* to the rock, on this occasion he was so provoked and angry in his spirit that he lost control of himself; and the result was that Moses lost faith: instead of speaking to the rock, he *struck* the rock once and twice; even so, God hallowed himself: in spite of what Moses did, God vindicated himself before His people by having graciously allowed the water to come forth in great abundance from the rock. Moses disobeyed God, but God vindicated himself by mercifully giving the people and their beasts water despite their complaint and murmuring.

Psalm 106 tells us that on this occasion Moses' spirit was so provoked that he spoke ill-advisedly with his lips (vv. 32-33). He was so angry that when he spoke to the people, he spoke rashly and declared: "All right, you rebels, shall I give you water to drink?"; and so Moses in anger struck the rock. By this action he failed to honor God and misrepresented Him in the sight of the people. Consequently, God said to Moses: "Because you did not believe Me, obey Me, and hallow Me before My people, therefore, you shall not lead them into the Promised Land" (Numbers 20:2-13).

Let us be clear here that this entire event is indicative of the fact of Moses' unbelief in God—he lost his faith. On this occasion he did not believe that by *speaking* to the rock water would come forth as had occurred previously. For on that previous occasion water had indeed come out of the rock when he struck it (Exodus 17:1-6); so he thought to be certain of the same outcome he would strike the rock a second time. Hence, having struck it once, he must have then thought that on this second occasion with the rock once was not going to be enough for the desired result to happen, so he struck it a second time. This was a definite indication of unbelief on Moses' part.

Let us understand that the staff Moses used to smite the rock was not his rod; it was Aaron's rod. God had said, "Take the staff from before My presence in the tabernacle—before the ark" (Numbers 20:7-9). That was Aaron's rod which had budded and blossomed and produced fruit and which had then been laid before the ark. In other words, Moses was instructed in *this* instance to exercise priestly authority before Jehovah God by speaking to Him and the water would most certainly come forth, because the rock had already been struck one time earlier. It thus did not need to be struck again. "Just speak," God had instructed, "and water will come forth" (20:8). But Moses did not believe God. So in his striking the rock with Aaron's rod its buds and flowers would all be damaged.

Now, according to Biblical typology, this event has great significance because the rock spoken of here is Christ himself. He is the Rock that had continually followed the children of Israel throughout their wilderness journey (I Corinthians 10:4); and because Christ was smitten on the cross once, water came forth; life came out of Him (John 19:14). This smiting of Christ at Calvary was done once and for all (Romans 6:10a). It is therefore not necessary to have Christ smitten—crucified—a second time in order to have life flow forth. Once and for all He was crucified for us. He was struck down for us that one time only and water came forth; life flowed out from Him. All we need to do when we want to enjoy His life is to speak by faith through our priestly function as priests to God (Exodus 19:6a, Revelation 1:6a). Take what He has already done once and for all and apprehend it; claim His redemptive work by faith and water will come forth—that is to say, life will flow again.

However, instead of believing, Moses acted terribly wrong because of unbelief. That was the only occasion in which Moses really did not believe; and because of that, he was not permitted to lead the people into the Promised Land (Numbers 20:12), and thus that work could not be done under his leadership. On other occasions, however, Moses may have sometimes wavered; he may have sometimes felt he could not continue on; sometimes, in fact, he wanted to give up; but when on all those occasions God assured him, he had always believed. And because of his faith in God and God's word, Moses was able to do God's work.

From this we realize that for us who are called to serve the Lord, faith is not only required in our spiritual life but also in our spiritual work. More often than not, of course, we recognize that we need to have faith for our spiritual life. As a matter of fact, without faith we could not even initially believe in the Lord Jesus (John 1:12, 3:15). We realize that we are saved by grace through faith (Ephesians 2:8). We realize that without faith how can we receive the grace of God? Therefore, we readily understand that faith is important; yet, not only is faith important at the beginning of our spiritual life, it is important throughout our entire spiritual life. It is a matter of continuing on from faith to faith (Romans 1:17 AV, ASV; cf. NIV). We must not only believe that Christ has borne our sins on Calvary's cross so that our sins may be forgiven, we must also believe that when Christ was crucified, our old man was crucified with Him in order for us to be delivered from the power of sin (Romans 6:6-7).

Now many believers have the faith to believe in Christ bearing our sins in His body on the cross and receiving the forgiveness of sins, but they do not have the faith to believe that Christ has already taken them onto the cross with Him so that no longer do *they* live but it is Christ who lives in and through them (Galatians 2:20). And because they do not believe, they do not experience the liberty of the sons of God.

If, however, you and I do believe, we need only to reckon ourselves as dead unto sin in Christ, reckon ourselves as alive to God in Christ, and we will live (Romans 6:11). It is all accomplished by faith: throughout our spiritual life it is simply a matter of faith, believing that God exists and believing that He is the Rewarder of all who seek after Him. We therefore need faith continually because without faith we cannot live out the spiritual life.

Paul wrote that "we [are to] walk by faith, not by sight" (II Corinthians 5:7). This is our spiritual life, but we are sometimes inclined to forget that faith is absolutely needed not only in the area of life but also in the area of work. Faith is very essential; indeed, it is fundamental. Without faith we cannot do God's work; yet many of God's people are working *for* Him but are not working *with* Him because that, too, requires faith. If we really want to do God's work, we have to believe.

I very much like that verse in John 6:29. It is a verse which many people probably overlook. The occasion on which the Lord Jesus uttered the words of that verse was when he multiplied those well-known five loaves and two fish to feed five thousand people. Those people were exceedingly happy because their food problem was solved, so that from their perspective there was no need in their lives to work anymore. At this moment, therefore, unemployment was not a problem for them because they had been supplied with food by the hand of the Lord; they therefore attempted to force Christ to become their King who would continually supply their every need. He, however, sent them away; but the very next day they came to Him again, thus moving the Lord Jesus to say to them: "You are not coming to Me because you witnessed that great sign; you are coming to Me because you want to be filled without having to labor anymore. But you will need to continue to labor. Yet I would say to you, labor not for the food that perishes, but work for the food that does not perish" (see John 6:27a). Immediately upon hearing these words of Jesus, the Jews present said, "Master, what must we do that we may work the works of God?" They here said that they wanted to work for God, but, they inquired, What must we do? And the Lord responded with the words of that verse 29 which I like very much: "This is the work of God, that ye believe on him [Christ] whom he [God] has sent."

What is God's work? What does "doing God's work" mean? The Jewish people of that day inquired in so many words as follows: "Now what should we do? We want to do something for God. Perhaps we can sacrifice something to Him or serve in some way or engage in some activities, or do something else for Him. Surely that would be doing His work." But the Lord said, "No; doing God's work is believing. Believe on the One whom God has sent." In other words, you and I must believe Christ. If we believe Him we are doing God's work because God's work can only be done by God's Son himself. And hence, if we believe Him, He is able to do His work in and through us, but if we do not believe Him, we ourselves are doing the work and not the Lord.

Do we discern the difference here? If faith is not involved in our spiritual work, it is not God's work. If the work does not require faith for its accomplishment but we ourselves can and do in fact do it, then we need to recognize that we are working *for* God but not working *with* God. It is not a doing of God's work at all because His work is essentially a work done by faith. It is quite true, of course, what the apostle James has written, that faith without works is dead; but let us realize that work done without faith is also dead. And hence, we need to be delivered from dead works (James 2:17-26). Faith is absolutely essential in doing God's work. Yet what do I mean by that?

1) It means, first of all, that if it is by faith by which we are doing the work, then God has to be the One to take the initiative. Briefly stated, therefore, the work cannot be originated from our

side. Even if we have the thought of doing something good, that too is a matter of us originating the work and not God. He must be the One to initiate that work.

2) If a work is being done by faith it means that the work must be done in God's way, not in our way.

3) If a work is being done by faith it means that the work must be done according to God's timing and not ours. We are always in a hurry. Recall that when Moses was forty, he assumed that that was the time to do God's work, but that work ended in failure because God knew that it was too early for the work to begin to be done through Moses. It is only when we have come to the end of ourselves that God's timing for His work to begin has arrived. We, on the other hand, are of the opinion that if we were to come to the end of ourselves, the opportunity to do God's work will be gone, so *we* must move forward and do it. But God's reaction will be: "No, you yourselves are doing the work. I myself am going to do it, but until you come to the end of yourselves the time for My work to be done through you shall never come."

4) If a work is being done by faith it means that it must be done according to His power and not according to our strength.

5) If a work is being done by faith it means that it must be done to His glory and not to ours.

So if a work is being done by faith in God, it will actually be that which is being accomplished by Him, through Him, and for Him—that is, for His glory. All the above points, therefore, comprise what I believe is a full definition of what it means for us to do God's work by faith.

So let us bear constantly in mind this one essential truth: If you really want to serve the Lord in whatever capacity it might be, in whatever area of work it might be, it has to be done by faith. Without faith no one can please God nor serve God. You must do the work by faith, looking off and away from yourself to Jesus, the Author and Finisher of your faith (Hebrews 12:2a). Otherwise, whatever so-called work of God you do will suffer.

Whenever our faith ceases, God's work through us ends; for if the work can be carried on when our faith falters or if the work can continue forward when our faith is totally lost, it is no longer God's work; it becomes our work and we are the ones doing it. Hence, faith is absolutely necessary; it is the essential ingredient in accomplishing God's work.

Thank God that Moses was a man of faith. Yet, though he clearly became a man of faith, his faith failed him at Meribah in the striking of the Rock instead of speaking to the Rock (see again Numbers 20:11-13). And this failure of his in faith is but one example among others to be found in the Bible of a person's strongest trait being the very point in that one's makeup wherein he or she falls. Indeed, it is quite strange that this is usually what happens. Not only was this the experience of Moses and others mentioned in Scripture but the same circumstance marks our own experience, does it not? That strongest commendable character trait of ours may often be the very point in which we fall; and because of that, we need to utterly cast ourselves upon the mercy of God.

I would have us turn our attention next to the second of those two issues or true servanthood characteristics we are considering together today—that of Moses' faithfulness. Yes, indeed, Moses served God with faith, he having fervently exercised belief in Him continually; but he also served God with faithfulness. Now faithfulness and faith are related but are somewhat different from each other. Faith is that which is exercised towards God, but faithfulness is that which is exercised towards the work which God has entrusted to us to do. Moses had faith in God and he was faithful in doing the work which God had entrusted him to perform.

In this very connection, that comment by the Holy Spirit recorded in Hebrews 3 is truly marvelous. There we read this Spirit-inspired word: "Moses was faithful in all his [God's] house" (v. 2b; cf. also Numbers 12:7).

The background to Numbers chapter 12 cited just now is as follows: Moses had led the children of Israel out of Egypt, across the Red Sea, and through the wilderness. And as was pointed out last time, as they began to move out and away from Mount Sinai towards the Promised Land, something most unpleasant occurred. Miriam, Moses' elder sister, conspired with Aaron, Moses' older brother. The leadership over the children of Israel was composed of these two brothers and their sister. Miriam was a prophetess; Aaron was the high priest; and Moses was the chief leader, but somehow there came into this picture a kind of jealousy which probably began with one woman's jealousy over another woman: Miriam became jealous of Moses' wife, Zipporah.

Miriam being an elder sister had taken care of the infant Moses when he had been hidden in an ark by his parents. Miriam, however, was the one who had watched over him after being placed in the ark; and from that moment forward there had developed a motherly attitude of an elder sister towards the much younger Moses. She had therefore ever afterwards wanted Moses to be under her; but later, Zipporah had come into his life. And quite naturally, Zipporah as Moses' wife now had much more of his affection; so Miriam had begun to be jealous of this other woman; so much so, in fact, that at one point Miriam had called Zipporah a Cushite woman. Factually speaking, she was not a Cushite, but perhaps because of her darker complexion Miriam used that circumstance to put Moses' wife down. And out of this personal jealousy, the emerging situation grew into a kind of conspiracy on the part of Miriam to influence Aaron her way. So much so that they together began to accuse Moses, with his sister declaring: "Does God speak to you alone, Moses? Does not God speak to us also? Why are you assuming a position above us?"

Actually Moses had been serving God very faithfully. He was simply doing what God had commanded him. He was not ambitious or arrogant but merely doing his duty as God's faithful servant, yet he was misunderstood. Thus Moses was not only unjustly accused by the Israelite camp as a whole but even by his sister and brother who by this time were probably the nearest surviving kin to him. Now when this accusation happened, Moses said nothing: he did not argue nor even explain but left the matter totally to God. And it was on this occasion that the Scriptures recorded the Spirit-inspired commentary that Moses was the meekest of all men upon the face of the earth (Numbers 12:3). And it was within this context that his meekness was particularly manifested, and God vindicated him.

Here is how God vindicated His faithful servant: He called Moses, Aaron and Miriam to the door of the tent of meeting and they together stood there. God who was very angry came down and said the following: "If there is any prophet among you, I will speak to that one in visions and in dreams. But not so with my servant Moses. He is faithful in all My house, and so I speak to him face to face. How, then, do you dare accuse him!" And God withdrew from them in anger. Now when the divine glory departed from these three, Aaron—who was the high priest, and because his eyes had been trained—saw immediately that Miriam's flesh had suddenly broken out with leprosy. So Aaron immediately pleaded with Moses and Moses pleaded with God, and God forgave and healed Miriam; but let us note in passing that the whole journey of God's people was delayed for seven days as a consequence (Numbers 12:14-15). Moses was faithful in all God's house, and if we want to serve God, faithfulness is absolutely essential.

In I Corinthians 4 the apostle Paul declared: "What is required of a steward is faithfulness" (see v.2). He went on to say this: "I do not mind if I am examined by you or by any man's court. I do not even examine myself because all such is nothing, but it is the Lord who examines me" (see vv.3-4 NIV, NASB). What is required of the servant of the Lord is faithfulness.

In what particular way was Moses faithful in all God's house? I think there is one portion of Scripture which demonstrates this fact more than anywhere else in the Bible and that is the lengthy narrative describing how he received from above the pattern for, and then built, the tabernacle. We may recall that when God commanded Moses while he was on Mount Sinai to build the tabernacle, He gave him the pattern to follow for its construction and for all its furnishings. Again and again Moses was warned by God that he should do everything according to the pattern which he had received when atop the mountain (e.g., 25:9, 40; cf. Hebrews 8:5b). Moses was told not to deviate or change anything but to do everything according to the pattern given to him there. And Moses built that tabernacle exactly according to the pattern shown him. I believe that that was where his great faithfulness was manifested.

We will recall that when Moses was in Egypt, he had learned all the learnings of Egypt which were to be absorbed. And it was mentioned before that Egypt at that period in history was the foremost empire in the entire world. And among her accomplishments Egypt was especially noted for its architectural feats. Even today when people visit the pyramids and observe the massive stones which were brought and then put together at such great heights and without all the modern technological and scientific inventions, they have had to acknowledge how perfect they all are. Hence, we can rightly conclude that Moses, having acquired such learning, must have been a great engineer, architect and builder. He could even contribute to the building up of an empire; so that, by comparison, for God to have instructed him to build a tabernacle was nothing. In fact, God could have very well simply told Moses: "Build Me a tabernacle," and he could have built one that would have been tremendous in size, gorgeous in beauty, and glorious in splendor. Moses would have known how to do it without any instruction having to be necessary. Indeed, from the human standpoint Moses' construction would probably have been much more massive, beautiful and glorious than the one for which God had given the pattern!

In light of this, I have sometimes thought that God's instruction was almost like an insult to Moses. God gave him all the details, what materials to use—even instructing him down to the very nails and threads—how much of everything to use, how to make this and that object, and where to put them. Everything was laid out in a pattern down to the very last detail, and God said repeatedly: "Moses, do not change any element but do it all according to My pattern."

Why did God warn Moses of this more than once? We may perhaps surmise that there must have been a temptation for Moses to make changes. It would only be natural for one who was such an accomplished architect, engineer and builder to take the blueprint in his hands, study it, and then think that it could be improved a little here and there and perhaps even enlarged. Can we therefore not see that this very temptation could have easily arisen in Moses' mind? God therefore warned him repeatedly: "Do not deviate from my pattern in any respect." And Moses was dutifully faithful in this regard—he rejected each and every temptation to change, improve, or alter any aspect or detail by faithfully following God's pattern down to the very last particular. Moses was indeed faithful in all God's house.

Why is this aspect of Moses' faithfulness so important? Let us take note of two thoughts expressed in Hebrews chapter 3 where it is said that "Moses … was faithful in all his [God's] house as a ministering servant." Thought number one: Moses was a servant and not a master. The passage goes on to say that Moses' faithfulness was "a testimony of the things to be spoken after" (v.5). This expresses the second thought, which perhaps requires a little explanation. We need to see that the tabernacle which God ordered Moses to build was but a shadow of that which was to come later. The tabernacle of old which was built according to the heavenly pattern actually served as a testimony of what was to come forth many, many centuries later. What, then, emerged as the reality of that shadow-testimony? In other words, what would be *the* tabernacle that would be coming forth much later? Is it not the church? Is not the church "the true tabernacle" (cf. Hebrews 8:2)?

Exodus records what God, referring to the tabernacle of that day, had declared: "This is my holy habitation, and I shall dwell in it" (see, e.g., 25:8; cf. Leviticus 26:11; Ephesians 2:22; Exodus 40:34). And the Lord Jesus announced to His disciples: "I will build my church" (Matthew 16:18a). God the Son would build the church for himself and for God His Father. And so we see that God's thought from eternity past to eternity future is that He wants to dwell among human beings: in the past, in the tabernacle; in the present, in the church; and in the ages to come, in New Jerusalem.

It is a wonderful reality, is it not, that the Father dwells in the Son and the Son dwells in the Father (cf. John 17:21a, 23a). There is a mutual dwelling in each other. The Father makes His Son His home and the Son makes the Father His home. They are always home to each other, and what a sweet home it is! Yet it is the will of God to extend that home to include us (see again John 17:21a; cf. Ephesians 2:2). God wants to live in us that we may live in Him. We are to be that tabernacle and that church in which He can dwell among us human beings forever.

But what kind of a dwelling place can God dwell in?—for even the heavens and the heaven of heavens cannot contain Him. God can only dwell in His Son (see once more John 17:21a, 23a). Did not God declare from heaven: "This is My beloved Son in whom I am well pleased, satisfied, and resting"? (see Matthew 3:17) God can only dwell in His Son, but it is the will of God that His Son should be the firstborn among many sons—among many brethren (Romans 8:29b, cf. Hebrews 12:23a). Therefore, the church—the tabernacle in reality—that God wants to build as His dwelling place must be built with Christ in you, in me, in all of us.

The church has to be built exclusively of Christ, and nothing but Christ. We cannot inject some foreign material into that dwelling place. We cannot add to it anything more than Christ nor can we take anything out of Christ from it. We cannot change anything. In other words, the church of God that He is building has to be built according to Christ and not according to doctrine, to creeds, to teachings, to forms, systems, or methods. It has to be built according to God's pattern which is the living Christ, the Christ whom God has revealed and whom we have confessed and experienced. It has to be Christ and nothing but Christ. And that is the reason why in building the tabernacle of old Moses had to do so most faithfully according to God's instructed pattern.

So, what is our pattern today? It is Christ. Our New Testament church pattern is not that which is according to elders and deacons. Our New Testament pattern of the church is not that which is according to the Apostolic creed, however good that may be. The pattern of the house of God today is solely according to the living Christ. And be it understood that it is not even according to the knowledge about Christ, but is according to Christ himself.

And that is where this matter of faithfulness comes into the picture. Are we faithful in all of God's house? Moses was only faithful in regard to shadows, but today we are working in accordance with the reality; therefore, how much more serious is it in our day than it was at the time of Moses; nevertheless, Moses was faithful in everything pertaining to God's house. Are we, like Moses, faithful? God is doing His work of building His church with and through people such as we are. Some of us may be like a foreman—as was Paul, who laid the foundation (I Corinthians 3:10a); but others of us may be like those who build upon the foundation (v. 10b). But regardless the category, we are all engaged in God's work; even so, the question remains to be honestly answered by each of us: How faithful are we? Are we building with gold, silver, and precious stones—that is to say, with the nature of God, the redemption of Christ, and the work of the Holy Spirit? Or are we building with wood, hay and stubble—that is to say, with our own life, our nature, and our own work: and all for our own glory? (vv.12-13a) Exactly on what foundation is it that we are building? Is it Christ? For the foundation laid must be Christ himself, as Paul went on to make clear (v.11). That is where faithfulness must truly come into focus. So let us realize that if we want to serve God we have to serve Him faithfully, and by being faithful it means that everything has to be according to the heavenly pattern, which is Christ.

Now the evidence of faithfulness is also to be seen and substantiated in the area of diligence. In this regard, if we are being faithful in doing God's work, it means that we are doing so diligently. Oh, do let us notice how diligent Moses was! In reading through the books of Exodus and Numbers, I do not believe anyone can say that Moses was lazy at any point in carrying out God's work. On the contrary, a person must acknowledge that Moses was a most diligent servant of God. Oh, how he labored incessantly! How he prayed! How he interceded! How he judged! How he led! Moses was most diligent in exercising whatever God had entrusted to him to accomplish. That too is an evidence of faithfulness which all who would be servants of God must manifest.

In Jesus' parable of the talents recorded in Matthew 25 we learn in figurative language that God gave to His servants talents according to their different abilities. One servant was given five talents, another, two talents, and a third was given one talent—all given according to each's particular ability. Thank God that He has made us all different! Not only do no two persons look alike, no two temperaments in them are exactly the same. The natural abilities which God has given us are all different, and this is in no way to be construed as signifying any inequality so far as people's created status as persons in the eyes of God is concerned. But in terms of natural abilities, God simply loves variety, that is all. Therefore, He makes us all different in that specific regard. And according to our different abilities God will give five talents, two talents, and one talent.

If you have greater gifts, more is required. If you have lesser gifts, less is required. If you have been given five talents and you earn five talents, you are approved by God as being diligent. If you have two talents and you earn two talents, you likewise are considered as being diligent. But if you have one talent and bury it, you fail to receive God's approval. Therefore, let us all trade—that is, let us all be diligent and function as members of the body of Christ according to the gift and grace which God has given to each of us (Romans 12:6a). Let us function accordingly. Every member is to do his or her part for the building up of the body of Christ in love (Ephesians 4:16). That is a manifestation of diligence; that is an evidence of faithfulness.

Finally, it is needful for me to point out that when we serve, we are always to do so with no ulterior motive. We are not to attempt to build a kingdom for ourselves; we are not to try to build a monument like to that of the tower of Babel of old (Genesis 11:1-9), but we are to build the house of God for Him to own and to occupy. In other words, faithfulness means we do all of God's work for Him and Him alone and not for ourselves.

So faith and faithfulness are the characteristics which we clearly see in the life of Moses in his serving God. And I do believe it is God's will and it is His desire that we who would serve Him in our generation (cf. Acts 13:36 NASB, NIV) would serve Him with both faith and faithfulness as did God's servant Moses.

Shall we pray:

Our heavenly Father, how we praise and thank Thee that we see in Thy servant Moses both faith and faithfulness. Our Father, we know that this is something which Thou dost require of all of us. We pray that we may always look away to Jesus, the Author and Finisher of our faith, so that everything we do is by faith. And our Father, if we should lose faith, we ask that Thou wilt stop us, so that we may return to Thee, look to Thee, and so that faith will be regained. And Father, we do also ask that we each may be faithful in whatever work which Thou hast committed to each and all of us. Oh, give all of us a vision of that heavenly pattern and teach us how by faith to receive it deeply, and faithfully fulfill it according to Thy will. And we want to give Thee all the glory. In the name of our Lord Jesus. Amen.

TITLES AVAILABLE
from Christian Fellowship Publishers

By Watchman Nee

- Aids to "Revelation"
- Amazing Grace
- Back to the Cross
- A Balanced Christian Life
- The Better Covenant
- The Body of Christ: A Reality
- The Character of God's Workman
- Christ the Sum of All Spiritual Things
- The Church and the Work – 3 Vols
- The Church in the Eternal Purpose of God
- "Come, Lord Jesus"
- The Communion of the Holy Spirit
- The Finest of the Wheat – Vol. 1
- The Finest of the Wheat – Vol. 2
- From Faith to Faith
- From Glory to Glory
- Full of Grace and Truth – Vol. 1
- Full of Grace and Truth – Vol. 2
- Gleanings in the Fields of Boaz
- The Glory of His Life
- God's Plan and the Overcomers
- God's Work
- Gospel Dialogue
- Grace Abounding
- Grace for Grace
- Heart-to-Heart Talks
- Interpreting Matthew
- Journeying towards the Spiritual
- The King and the Kingdom of Heaven
- The Latent Power of the Soul
- Let Us Pray
- The Life That Wins
- The Lord My Portion
- The Messenger of the Cross
- The Ministry of God's Word
- My Spiritual Journey
- The Mystery of Creation
- Powerful According to God
- Practical Issues of This Life
- The Prayer Ministry of the Church
- The Release of the Spirit
- Revive Thy Work
- The Salvation of the Soul
- The Secret of Christian Living
- Serve in Spirit
- The Spirit of Judgment
- The Spirit of the Gospel
- The Spirit of Wisdom and Revelation
- Spiritual Authority
- Spiritual Discernment
- Spiritual Exercise
- Spiritual Knowledge
- The Spiritual Man
- Spiritual Reality or Obsession
- Take Heed
- The Testimony of God
- The Universal Priesthood of Believers
- Whom Shall I Send?
- The Word of the Cross
- Worship God
- Ye Search the Scriptures

The Basic Lesson Series

- Vol. 1 - A Living Sacrifice
- Vol. 2 - The Good Confession
- Vol. 3 - Assembling Together
- Vol. 4 - Not I, But Christ
- Vol. 5 - Do All to the Glory of God
- Vol. 6 - Love One Another

TITLES AVAILABLE
from Christian Fellowship Publishers

By Stephen Kaung

Abiding in God
"But We See Jesus"—*the Life of the Lord Jesus*
Discipled to Christ—*As Seen in the Life of Simon Peter*
God's Purpose for the Family
The Gymnasium of Christ
In the Footsteps of Christ
The Key to "Revelation" – Vol. 1
The Key to "Revelation" – Vol. 2
Men After God's Own Heart—*Eight Biographies from the Book of Genesis*
Moses, the Servant of God
New Covenant Living & Ministry
Now We See the Church—*the Life of the Church, the Body of Christ*
Shepherding
The Songs of Degrees—*Meditations on Fifteen Psalms*
The Splendor of His Ways—*Seeing the Lord's End in Job*

<u>The "God Has Spoken" Series</u>
Seeing Christ in the Old Testament, Part One
Seeing Christ in the Old Testament, Part Two
Seeing Christ in the New Testament